D0679853

HELEN VAN PELT WILSON'S
OWN GARDEN
AND
LANDSCAPE BOOK

Helen Van Pelt Wilson's *OWN GARDEN AND LANDSCAPE BOOK*

Photographs by George Taloumis
except as noted

WEATHERVANE BOOKS • NEW YORK

Library of Congress Catalog Card Number: 72-89355

This edition is published by Weathervane Books
a division of Imprint Society, Inc., Distributed by Crown Publishers, Inc.
by arrangement with Doubleday & Company, Inc.
a b c d e f g h
Manufactured in the United States of America

For

Ruth Wyeth Spears

whose garden wisdom has been

so generously shared through the years

Contents

Charts and Lists

With many thanks

To George Taloumis, a skilled photographer, who "sees" plants and experiences beauty before he photographs.

To Charles Marden Fitch for his sensitive photographs that reflect his thorough knowledge of plants and their habitats.

To Walter J. Haring for the many fine color photographs he has taken of my garden.

To Peter C. Krieg, my young college friend, whose photographs are published for the first time in these pages.

To Dorothy C. Stemler for letting me use photographs of beautiful old-fashioned roses from her catalogue of *Tillotson's Roses.*

To Eloise A. Ray, L.A., who has measured this property and drawn the endpaper maps; she has also increased my knowledge of design.

To Lucy Sargent, my dear friend, who has shared her extensive knowledge of herbs with me.

To Edna J. Payne who helped me develop the iris list and is unhappy that I no longer plant German iris. She has also shared her wisdom on lilies and hemerocallis.

To Elizabeth B. Parry who knows and grows both roses and lilies skillfully, and agrees with me on lawns.

To F. Gordon Foster whose vast knowledge of ferns has made them even more delightful for me, and for his careful reading of my fern chapter.

To Peter J. Hannan whose Service keeps my planted place well pruned and free of pest and disease and who has helped me develop these control schedules.

To Joseph J. Maisano, Jr., Extension Agent for Western Connecticut, who has advised me on garden and lawn problems for a number of years.

To John W. Oliver, Jr., of the Oliver Nurseries, who has advised me on evergreens and azaleas.

To William L. Meacham, Managing Editor of *Home Garden,* for permission to use material that appeared in that magazine over the years.

To Rachel Snyder, Editor-in-Chief of *Flower Grower,* for permitting me to draw on articles I had written for that magazine about my planted place.

To Donald Wyman for making available to us in his *Gardening Encyclopedia* the new authoritative plant names from the manuscript being prepared for *Hortus III* by the Bailey Hortorium at Cornell University.

To Daniel T. Walden whose critical reading of my manuscript and wise counsel have been invaluable.

To Helen B. Krieg who has again cheerfully seen me through the inevitable crises of book preparation.

My Joys of Gardening

Since this book has been written on what might be termed a garden anniversary—my twentieth year here at Stony Brook Cottage—I'd like to offer my garden credo, thoughts on the joys that have come to me through gardening not only here but through the earlier years of tending plants elsewhere. Except for the advent of my sister in times when a new baby was a surprise and not an expectation, I really have no memories earlier than my ritual St. Patrick's Day planting of sweet peas in the clay soil along the house wall. I must have been about seven years old. I still recall the delight those spindly plants brought me, blooming despite New Jersey summer heat, and they were only the beginning. As Bacon noted, "Gardening is the purest of human pleasures," and so it has been with me.

One great joy, I think, is being able to be alone but not lonely in a garden. We all experience loneliness, and we need to find ways to cope with this human predicament. I've been lonely in a New York apartment without a place for plants but never in my Connecticut garden. Women, often more isolated than men, faced with "the empty nest" and perhaps twenty or more years of being alone ahead of them can find in a garden, as I have, a delightful consuming preoccupation. The plants you tend become the companions that need you, they mitigate the early evening hours, surely the loneliest time of day; they welcome your return after an absence. Suitcases upstairs, I've found myself, after a trip, clipping off dead blooms, pulling weeds, turning on sprinklers, sentimentally assuring my garden I'm home, and all this still in travel clothes—and my best shoes!

However you may enjoy being alone, gardening can also lead to the joy of association, as witness the tremendous membership of the

Federated Garden Clubs and that of the special plant groups like the African-violet societies. In these enthusiasm can be shared. And all gates are opened to the traveling gardener. Lean over a fence to admire an Englishman's delphiniums, and next thing you know you are drinking tea in his parlor.

But escape from the world and a place of silence are other joys. Working among his roses a businessman can untie his day; a housewife, sowing seeds in the lovely early days of spring, gets away for a little while from the eternities of housework, then returns to them refreshed. I frankly use my garden to escape people, even valued old friends whose flow of words today is "ceasing never." Sometimes I retreat to the end of the Fern Garden to pull goutweed in the sun while my house guests in the shade work up new topics. Of course, I have no telephone extension in my garden, as some do. How escape if I must drop the spade to lift the receiver!

I would not thus split the lovely sound of silence in my garden where I hear only nature's music; the song of birds, the brook conversing over the stones, the breeze sighing through the pines, rustling through the poplars. Of silence so little remains in this world of roaring airplanes and highways, piped-in music in elevators, at the hairdressers, even in banks, everywhere the incessant chatter of radio and T.V.

From a garden comes health of body and mind. You keep limber there, heaven knows, and gardening isn't like games that require club membership, and special garments and equipment; all you need is old clothes and plenty of old shoes, at least six pairs a season, easily acquired by making your new ones old as you simply forget to change.

Trivial annoyances slough off in a garden and problems often solve themselves there as you weed and plant. Gardening is such satisfyingly creative work, too; you can see the beautiful results of your efforts, not like the frustration of a poor golf score.

Perhaps it is the solace a garden offers that has meant the most to me. "All my hurts my garden spade can heal," Emerson claimed, but a garden does more than heal small hurts; it offers comfort in times of overwhelming sorrow. At least three times in my life I have turned to my garden in agony of spirit. The night after my sister's death the fragrant white lilies in the moonlight she would never see again gave me mystical assurance that she lived on in beauty. After I lost my son I relentlessly cultivated my garden. Returning from the hospital after a dear friend's death, I recall how I rejected the consolation of friends and drew close to the eternal verities of nature—my great rock ledge supporting giant oaks that had survived human suffering for centuries, the ancient apple tree, gnarled but enduring. I drew comfort from the trees I had set out a decade before, leaning my forehead against the tall trunks so much stronger than I that grievous day. I walked through the Fern Garden I had planted, past the brook to the steep meadow paths I had made.

My garden did not fail me then, nor in the bitter weeks that followed. I believe a garden never fails one who has worked long in it and becomes deeply associated with its beauty. I hope that your garden or your planted place will bring you the joy and solace that mine has brought me. I often think of Job's words, "Speak to the earth and it shall teach thee," and I *know* Job was right.

Helen Van Pelt Wilson
Stony Brook Cottage
Westport, Connecticut

HELEN VAN PELT WILSON'S
OWN GARDEN
AND
LANDSCAPE BOOK

Twenty years ago this is what I bought, a lively brook flowing along the west side of the property, cool in summer, exciting all year. Stiles photo.

1. STONY-BROOK COTTAGE BECOMES MINE

Concerning Real Estate, Velvet Turf, and Helpers

One way to get exactly the property you want is to do as I did. First, put down a sizable advance payment on a house and lot that don't quite suit you. Then returning to your city apartment, give in to a habit, now firmly entrenched, of reading real estate ads in the paper. There you may see a description of a place with a "rushing brook." This will be too much for you, so next day you will come out again to the country and investigate this irresistible brook. And so it will prove. When some twenty years ago I first considered this property, I was immediately charmed not only by the brook but by the ancient apple tree and the New England stone fences. The cliff above the brook was hidden by a sapling-covered dump so I didn't discover this treasure until I moved in, nor did I know that a straight 100-foot wild cherry grew opposite the terrace until I found a snow of petals on the grass the next spring.

I saw opportunity for many kinds of gardening on this acre plus. The land went gently up the hill over an old orchard in back and in front rose sharply to the country road. In the valley between stood the small house. Had I my wits about me I would have observed an

On a cold sunny day of snow, the brook sparkles as it flows fast under the bridge toward Long Island Sound. In times of flood, the water rises high enough to dash little waves against the boards and on that day the mail is not collected from the box above. Krieg photo.

ominous water line in the cellar and that there were no walks, no screens, and very little shade for the house. But none of these drawbacks filtered through my euphoria. The house was simply a necessary extra. I *had* to have the brook. Gone was my first deposit and gone my good sense. This never returned, for several years later I added to the original acre another acre, which I told myself was "for protection." I put a 15-inch snow fence along the old property line to keep me from expanding. What a delusion! I easily stepped over that fence and in due course put in the Fern Garden and the Round Garden on the new acre. Furthermore, I landscaped the back hill and finally laid out the Cliff Path in front.

On my first acre I had the invaluable assistance of Margaret Baillie, a landscape architect, who placed the important pink crab-apple trees that now frame the first glimpse of the house. She also straightened out the driveway to give me room for what is now my Look-Into Garden. This is wider than first planned and most of what was in it has outgrown the space and been transferred elsewhere. I recall that she particularly asked me if I wanted a close planting there for immediate effect, which unfortunately I did, rather than an open planting for the future. At that time the crab apple that the previous owner had planted was just the same height as I am, about five feet. Transplanted, it is now the handsome, 15-foot sculptured tree that accents the corner of the driveway.

In the early years here I was so intoxicated by opportunity, that despite the warnings of Mrs. Baillie, I extended and extended even to the point of planting a perennial border 10 feet deep by 70 feet long to follow the stone fence on the north. Today this area is mainly grass and the perennial border has become the limited Apple-Tree Garden. After twenty years with much less garden help than ever before, I have consistently cut down. It used to be that I would point and a gardener would dig. Now, I drive in the stake and do the digging myself. I have become a yard boy rather than a lady gardener. This solitary effort has caused me to reduce my grand ideas, and I am pleased to say that this year the work here is less than it has ever been, and I think the effect is better. I realize that this is partly due to the fact that this is now an old garden or, as I prefer to call it, a planted place. But the introduction of shrubs in the Fern Garden and elsewhere has meant less weeding, and great sweeps of groundcover have mitigated lawn headaches.

I wasn't aware of this great cliff on the west at the time of purchase, for it was hidden by a dump and a thick stand of saplings. With the trash cleared away and the trees thinned and pruned, the cliff dominates my black-and-white winter world, one of the treasures of this place. Krieg photo.

Lawns for the Planted Place—Superficial Approach to Velvet Turf

One of my first—and last—*mighty* efforts was the development of a fine lawn. I realize now that a lawn is the most time-consuming and least-rewarding aspect of any planted property. From early spring to late fall it needs *something*—fertilizing, seeding, reseeding, refertilizing, crabgrass control, weed-killers, maybe pest-or-disease controls plus the eternal mowing. I once figured my lawn had cost me $100 per square foot and even then it wasn't the greatest. It was routine for me to have the poor patches thoroughly renovated in spring; it wasn't until mid-June that the place was evenly green again.

The fact is "velvet turf" is a mirage in this country, an advertiser's dream but the home-owner's nightmare. We have inherited our green concept from the British. They have fine lawns because they have the proper climate for them. We don't. I almost never see a really good lawn here except an occasional small plot, usually hand-tended by a retired person with infinite time and patience, someone whose lawn is his hobby. It certainly isn't mine and I've been a happier gardener since I stopped trying so hard and put my effort where it counted more. In fact, I'm not above conceding that if a lawn looks pretty good at a 12-foot glance, that lawn looks good enough.

Here's what I do now:

Early in April, I fertilize heavily, lightly again in late August or early September, depending on the rain, with a slow-release organic material, high in nitrogen, of course. Fertilizing in July is often recommended but at that time here, drought often sets in so I wait.

Also in April any really bad spots are lightly scratched and seed sown—no great renovation though. In fall, the whole lawn is overseeded with as good a seed mixture as I can afford.

Now about seed. There is no question about it, a worthwhile mixture is expensive. It will contain very little annual rye which is all right as a starter or "nurse grass" but the plants don't last. A good mixture will be made up mainly of Kentucky Bluegrass (but not entirely because this naturally turns brown in summer unless faithfully watered) and fescues. Fescues thrive in sun, not just in shade as is commonly supposed; I *do* sow fescue seed alone in the shadier areas here. Of course, no grass will grow in deep shade.

To the grass mixture, I add about a fifth of white clover seed. This is heresy to the purists who apply special weed-killers to get rid of clover. However, clover is consistently green in sun and shade, resists

This is the cottage that came along with the brook; I didn't pay much attention to it or consider its deficiencies until I moved in. Wells photo.

Stony Brook Cottage, twenty years later, with every wall knocked out for new windows, the roof raised, a new kitchen, an arbor built, and shade trees planted for summer comfort. Bradbury photo.

chinch bug, and also fungus attacks. In the humid conditions—caused here by shade and the brook—bacterial disease is an ever-present threat. Some yellow spots usually develop in July; I overlook them and don't spray, as perhaps I should, but fall seeding and fertilizing take care of the trouble to a satisfactory degree.

I don't apply any weed-killers. Believe it or not, in spring I enjoy digging out dandelions and other broadleaf weeds with an asparagus knife, and with a feeding weeds and crabgrass tend to disappear.

Finally I keep the lawn well watered in times of summer drought so it stays green. The mower is set at 2 inches, no scalping, and if the grass doesn't need mowing because it isn't growing much when there is no rain for weeks, we skip cutting. Too often if you have a Mowing Service, your grass is cut on a weekly schedule and at times when it needs longer growth to protect the roots from heat and drought.

Obviously I am no lawn specialist, only an experienced and cynical amateur. Libraries teem with books on "easy" lawn procedures but the word "easy" in connection with lawns nauseates me. Actually my limited unchemical procedures have produced as satisfactory a lawn as I have ever had, and my resolution to stop trying to grow grass where grass obviously does not care to grow has been a good one. There the extension of groundcover has rescued me.

About groundcovers, I will have more to say later in this book. Suffice to remark now that in these times with the scarcity and cost of help, you too may do well to adopt my lawn philosophy and to follow my plan for a *planted place* rather than a highly *gardened* property. Flowers—annuals, perennials, and bulbs—can be used mainly for accent or in one or two small colorful masses, as in my Apple-Tree and Look-Into Gardens. There they give the best possible colorful effect for the least effort. I also depend on flowering shrubs and trees. Although I no longer have those beautiful, but so demanding, perennial borders, or a formal rose garden, or impressive sweeps of lawn, I am pleased with this less-exacting informality and the new look of my planted place, and I think you may like such a change too. After all, our properties are for our pleasure and comfort nor further opportunity for character development.

Some Helpers I Have Had

I am a firm believer in engaging a certified professional to protect my trees and shrubs from pests and diseases. If you don't have too big a place—I am coping with more than two acres—you may be able to manage this yourself but it takes both strength and know-how to protect laurel at the right time from lace bugs, birches from leaf-miner, and evergreens from mites. I know I couldn't fight inchworms on my own; and I am well aware that the many towns here that have tried to avoid spraying altogether—and for good reason—have had to compromise. Anyway, I want regular protection, not clean-up, by a qualified man who has my place on his schedule and shows up without frantic telephone calls from me.

In my case the same qualified person does the pruning which, especially for big trees, is much too important to leave to just anyone who can hack with a saw. If you take the time to understand the business of pruning, you can do a great deal of it yourself. Men usually enjoy this task, but if they do, you have to watch that they aren't carried away (especially if they're mad about something and taking it out with indiscriminate whacking; I once saw a crab apple practically reduced to the ground under these circumstances).

For advice appropriate to your locality, you will find a government agricultural service listed in your telephone book. To locate this, you must search diligently. The name of the service you want may be hidden not simply under a county or state name but as: cooperative, extension, university, college, school of agriculture, even institute. So, persevere. For you, as a home gardener, it is well worth while to know where to get professional help. You can have your soil tested and get advice on exactly how to improve it (free or for a small fee), and find out just what trees, shrubs, and so on are best suited to *your* locality. I find my county agent's monthly news letter, *Gardening Ideas,* an invaluable guide.

I suggest you avoid *most* of the firms with trucks labeled "Garden Specialist" or even "Complete Landscaping Service." Too often their aim is to sell you plants, fertilizer, weed-killers, even "top soil" that may have come from the bottom of somewhere. The Lawn Advisers are the worst; they always want to start by plowing up the whole thing. A good way to check on them is to ask to see some local lawn they have successfully planted and managed for at least a year; they could never show me one. Better be your own yard boy, as I am, than depend on these.

In the matter of helpers, my experience has been long, rich, and deep. Since the passing of the "regular" gardener, a man who came daily, loved plants, and knew what he was doing, I have alternated between services that usually included a boss and four to five workers who descended like locusts to mow and weed my place and didn't have a clue except with bills, which were tremendous. The team always included a brother or nephew, the most ignorant of the lot. One such tore out a big spread of cherished winter aconites but "they looked like weeds," another uprooted most of my groundcover of sweet woodruff along the Cliff Path for the same reason. When I remonstrated at such mayhem at $4.00 per hour, I was told, "But he's my brother, he's just a boy."

Another helper didn't even recognize a violet but "he was good with machines." Actually they all are good with machines, particularly mowers they can sit on, or electric equipment requiring little muscle. If they know even a little about pruning, they will inform you they are "tree men," and can't cut down a meadow with scythes because they get blisters. In general, boys suffer extremely from heat and bolt at the first sign of rain, though they are unconscious of a soaking while watching football. Peter, a really good high school helper, to give interest to his work, mowed my initials on the lawn. Kim measured the whole property and tacked up the figures in the garage to help me estimate amounts of fertilizer for each area. He also printed the names of the tools on the garage wall to indicate proper storage spots. When he went off to college, he left written directions for the next boy that described locations, as the Round Garden, the Fern Garden, and other places that he knew I'd talk about. I missed Kim very much.

Bill, a very thorough helper, triumphantly removed every smidgen of the ubiquitous goutweed from the Fern Garden. I couldn't believe it; for a full week we were free of it! And this has never happened since. Mark read me the love sonnets he wrote to his girl, and they were certainly a far cry from the Lucy poems. Most of my helpers had to take cola breaks, and also required bathroom privileges. In general they have been a cheerful lot if not pressed, or expected to work as hard as I do or as fast. Generally, they are bored and want company; for them gardening is a lonely business.

A long line of high school boys has now come and gone. I have trained many a future husband for outdoor suburban tasks; his wife, if she ever knows, should bless me. The best, and eventually most knowledgeable, boys graduate too soon and disappear.

My last notable experience occurred in the summer of the "English major." Not even by stretching the connotation could this married college student be called a gardener. His first day he queried, "What's a spade?" He informed me that literature, not the soil, was his milieu; at lunch time he borrowed the New York *Times* Book Review and had a long read and rest. However, he had never heard of Wordsworth but thought he was "in the course next semester." The climax came when Tom lost a watch, borrowed, he said, to time his wife's forthcoming labor pains in the modern manner. We searched for hours among plants and baskets of weeds—to no avail. In due course he telephoned; the watch was located before the time of need "in the pocket of my other pants." Now he brings the baby to see me and tells me he is thinking of giving up college because the president "has no idea how to run the place." This English major, who had trouble with the simplest automatic equipment, now wants to work with his hands, perhaps woodcarving, making bowls and such for a living. Remembering, I wonder!

My gardening life has now fallen in pleasant places. Groundcovers and other work-savers have reduced the burden and I have found a neighbor, Jerry Tuccinardi, with the Italian's characteristic love of growing things. He has an after-work mowing service with a small crew, and he really understands both lawns and plants. He gardens with me once a week for three or four hours, late afternoon to evening. We labor together with mutual respect and in political amity—we are both fighting the location of a garbage transferral site near us. Jerry worries over how hard I work in the heat on this place; he sympathizes with my suffering from wasp and mosquito bites. I am sorry for the long and very early hours of his regular job, and mindful of his fatigue when he finally comes to me. We both hate goutweed and admire azaleas tremendously. My fingers are crossed!

Early in spring, 'King Alfred' daffodils open in golden abundance in the shelter of the cliff. Raymond photo.

The sunset is seen through the old elms, maples, and a wild cherry on the banks of the brook; an awning—up in spring, down in fall, stored in winter—sheltered the terrace before the hawthorn was planted close to the house. Stiles photo.

2. *BIG TREES AND OTHER SHADY PROCEDURES*

How to Have Comfort —and Flowers Too

On any property, shade is essential, the degree, a matter of the owner's preference, for shade can be regulated. Even if you have built a house in the woods, you need not fully accept the natural situation, but how many trees you cut down or how much you thin them out should be a matter of pretty careful consideration, also how many more you plant if some of your favorites are missing.

When I came to Stony Brook Cottage, the sun poured down unmercifully, east, south, and west. This was a blessing in winter but most uncomfortable in summer. At the start, I put up awnings south and east and on the west an awning canopy over an open terrace. How I came to loathe those awnings—up in spring, down in fall, stored in winter, and after two years not the color they started with. What I needed was more trees, close to the house. The handsome elms by the brook, old maples, beech, sassafras, and the balm-of-Gilead on the outer reaches of the property did not cool the house indoors. What I needed were big deciduous trees on the east and south as protection from summer glare, and as many of the smaller deciduous trees as was practical—or maybe a few more because I like them. These medium-height trees too, say, 25 feet, placed close enough to shade but not in maturity to smother, have delighted me through the years. (My favorites are described in the next chapter.) Of course, I wanted the shifting shade of fairly open foliage, not the density of catalpa. For big deciduous trees I chose an ash and a sweet-gum, and one big true white birch, the European *Betula pendula,* and later as the elms had to go because of disease, I set in their places beside the brook a tulip-tree for nostalgic reasons, and an open lacy zelkova.

I have also removed a number of trees, mostly across the brook, but always working toward my ideal of a home with plenty of morning sun in winter, especially to breakfast by, and with afternoon shade to ease the heat of summer. I love the long cool shadows cast by trees on a hot afternoon. Because so many trees are dear to me, I've always found it difficult to be restrained, but there should be limits to the amount of shade that is permitted. Too much means a dank dim house; too little, unmitigated glare and fading of wallpaper and upholstery. The home of one friend is so densely shaded by ancestral hemlocks (I think they were originally part of an ill-chosen foundation planting), that the electric light is almost always on in the living room! I'd take an axe to those hemlocks tomorrow, for a sunless house is a gloomy house and not conducive to a cheerful spirit. Another home is so sun-drenched that blinds are kept drawn all summer. I never return from a visit there without blessing again my own big shade trees.

It is usual to speak of the "problems of shade." For me they do not exist. Gardening in the shade is one kind of gardening; gardening in the sun, another. Neither is a matter of problems but of procedures. You do things differently; the emphasis is not the same. Certainly the plants are different. Here are some of my shady procedures that you may wish to follow:

Judicious Tree Planting. First decide exactly where you want sun protection. Study the slant of the sun on a bright day. Does it leave the terrace vulnerable, the living room unlivable in the afternoon, the upstairs too hot for a nap? But perhaps you want more sun than I do. I'd always prefer the screened and shaded porch to the blazing beach, but maybe you wouldn't. Perhaps you want a sun trap, a corner of a patio or small unplanted area protected from wind and large enough for a long beach chair. In this case, consider your own

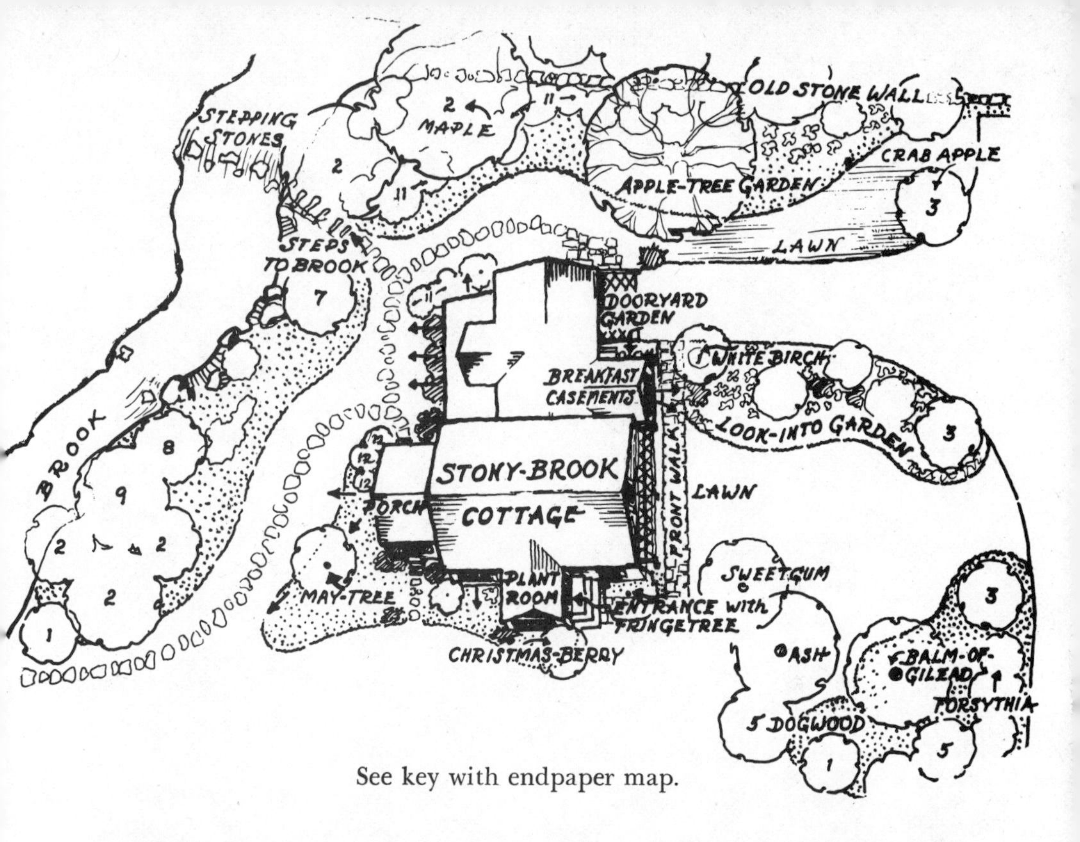

See key with endpaper map.

preference as you plan. On a small place, say a 60-by-100-foot lot, one big tree and perhaps two or three smaller ones should be your limit. On an acre or so, you can have more. Allow the big trees—oaks, sweet-gums, maples—about a 30-foot spread; smaller flowering trees about 15 feet each. In this regard I hope you will do as I say, not as I have done. Because of unbridled enthusiasm, I have planted too close. If in the years ahead crowding becomes unbearable, I hope someone else will have to cope not me. The chart of big trees at the end of this chapter and the one of smaller trees following Chapter 3 include some of my favorites that you may like too.

Removal of Some Trees. The woodman-spare-that-tree people consider it sacrilegious ever to get rid of a tree no matter how it darkens a house. One year I took out ten trees mostly across the brook and more are destined to go in the course of time. Before removing them, I have studied their contribution and tried to imagine what opening up each area would do. Invariably there is improvement, perhaps a new view of the brook, less clutter in front of my serene rock ledge, more chance for a fine lawn specimen previously lost in competition, or maybe just more light and air for the house. In other words, shady gardening needs to be selective.

Shaded by a tall English May-tree, a hawthorn, pruned high and open, the enclosed porch is screened from the western sun and is cool and comfortable through summer heat. A grass path associates the Fern Garden in the foreground with the open lawn around the house.

1. In May the Apple-Tree Garden is full of flowers; beyond, *Viburnum carlesii* is covered with clove-scented coral brooches, and the tall pink crab apple beside the driveway is a great cloud of double pink blossoms. *Haring photo.* 2. LEFT. Dogwoods glisten in the sun along the southern boundary of the lawn. 3. RIGHT. Well-pruned golden forsythia lights the still wintry landscape and a tapestry of red tulips, dark blue scillas, and white hyacinths, all early bulbs, brings to life the end of the Look-Into Garden. *Fitch photos.*

4. Along the driveway, following peony bloom there, spectacular pink 'Evelyn Claar' daylilies open in the Look-Into Garden, bringing color throughout July. 5. BELOW. In the dooryard garden beside the kitchen steps, pink impatiens blooms all summer at the feet of St. Francis; the potted chrysanthemums are introduced for autumn color. *Taloumis photos.*

6. In the early fall sunshine, chrysanthemums make a garden at the front door. 7. LEFT. Impatiens blooms freely in the shade of the white birch in the Look-Into Garden. *Taloumis photos.* 8. RIGHT. A maple pruned to sculptured form makes a background for the Round Garden. *Haring photo.*

9. In full view through the plant-room window and from the indoor staircase, azaleas—white, pink, and yellow—make a glorious May-June picture in association with hemlocks, laurel, and birch, all underplanted with pachysandra. *Fitch photo.*

10. A May view of Stony Brook Cottage from the top of the east hill through the pair of small pink crab apples along the driveway; at the right, the tall crab apple and apple tree both in full bloom. *Ricau photo.*

High and Drastic Pruning. On a predominately shady property, it's a good idea to keep trees in hand both as to density and branch height. High shade, not too thick, so that sun and light can filter through and permit a wide variety of plants to grow under branches is my aim, especially for the doorstep plantings. Above my Fern Garden, the wild cherry and the volunteering oak are permitted no low branches. Here and elsewhere these are regularly removed when the spring rush gives me a breather and I can *think* about the picture I want.

I never allow trees growing close to the house to thicken up with low, shrubby growth that closes me in. I like to see the clear silhouette of a trunk, no suckers at the base, no weak foliage along the trunks. From the porch I want to look *through* bare twisted trunks to the flowing brook. I want to view across the brook the ledge revealed through the trunks of small high-pruned maples and beeches, a pleasing design of horizontal rock and perpendicular trunks. (Pruning is a subject covered in detail in Chapter 14.)

Regular Fertilizing and Watering. Plants in shade may be in competition with tree roots for food and moisture, and it is up to you not to let the battle get desperate. One spring I neglected to fertilize my heavily mulched Apple-Tree Garden, and the next year bleeding-hearts and bulbs there made a poor show. A good procedure for shaded plantings is *heavy* spring fertilizing *every* year for flowers and bulbs, and say monthly, but light feedings, for lawn areas directly under trees, this along with the usual spring and late summer fertilizing of the lawn as a whole. Then there needs to be *deep* watering in times of drought. By this I mean a slow-running hose at the roots of trees and big shrubs for two hours or more in each place and lawn sprinklers on for hours and moved about every hour. When there is no *heavy* rain, such watering should usually be repeated at weekly intervals. (More on watering in the Voice of Experience.)

Because they are competing with the roots of trees and shrubs, plants in shade need more than an average amount of nourishment. I save wood ashes from the fireplace for its rich potash content, spreading it in spring around roses, lilacs, peonies, and other plants that don't require acidity. The ashes must be kept covered till used; leached by water, they lose value. And I keep the compost coming. On a shady place, you never need look for the next load of leaves for compost but are overpowered with autumn abundance. I spread the coarser stuff as keep-down weed mulch under shrubs, and sprinkle the finer stuff, pressed through a half-inch sieve, as a feeding mulch over flower beds and thin lawn spots. You just can't have too much compost to feed and mulch your garden, and to keep it cool and weedfree in summer. Composting is, in fact, one of my favorite shady procedures.

Selecting the Right Plants. Those who see shade as a problem claim their choice of plants is limited. Yet if I made a list of all the plants that flourish here in shade, it would cover pages. Indeed I feel in no wise deprived by shade, but then I want only a few annuals, and I like the shade-tolerant kinds rather than marigolds and zinnias, handsome as these are in sun. Nor have I any pressing desire in hot weather for dahlias, gladiolus, or most of the other summer perennials that are sun-demanding.

In this climate of hot Julys and Augusts, it's the spring things I find most rewarding—bleedinghearts, mertensia, Jacob's-ladder, forget-me-nots, anchusa, coralbells, hardy candytuft, arabis, primroses, white violets, pansies that are sometimes winter-hardy, wild blue phlox and many other wildings, beside the ferns that I plant everywhere possible. Christmas roses thrive under an open-branched tree; specio-

Contrasting patterns of mountain-laurel, witch-hazel, and Christmas ferns are emphasized in the shifting light of old trees. On the ground, birds—made by the sculptor Dorothy Riester—are the keynote to this little sanctuary where real birds bathe in the cool water of a bath made by a big flower-pot saucer set on a stump which serves as pedestal. Bradbury photo.

sum and other lilies and purple and white platycodon do well in light shade. Of course, hundreds and hundreds of bulbs bloom here, mostly narcissus because they are so undemanding, but tulips too (though I give them as much sun as possible), and snowdrops, crocuses, hyacinths, scillas, and aconites. Aconites thrive in the unrelieved summer shade of a crab apple, also under lilacs below the living-room window where I can enjoy them in late February or early March without going outside. In an earlier garden, I had a copper beech with a yearly returning carpet of blue and white scillas beneath it. What a sight that was!

Except in the Look-Into Garden, late summer for me is mainly green and quiet with pale yellow daylilies, a few white hostas, sometimes tuberous begonias, the indispensable impatiens (lots of it), and flowering tobacco providing enough color. For fall, there are chrysanthemums, plants bought in heavy bud; at that point of development, flowers open well even under trees. Then there are the astilbes or spiraeas. If you don't know these shade-loving, completely reliable, fragrant perennials of fine foliage for early summer, do seek them out. My preference is one of the whites, 'Avalanche' or 'Deutschland', but several years ago in the botanical garden at Nymphenburg outside Munich in West Germany, I saw an extensive collection, perhaps fifty kinds, from little fellows to giants, from the meadow goatsbeard to obvious sophisticates. All were thriving under high shade, and all I could reach to smell were fragrant. Astilbes multiply rapidly and never get anything. They can be the shady gardener's dear friend. Also the daylilies. I have one planting of dark red ones with white astilbes in deep shade with ferns beside a pine tree and both perennials really bloom.

Minor Shady Matters. In your plantings, keep in mind that nature abhors a vacuum and that it's better for you to fill in with some desirable plants that will grow even in the deepest natural shade, as pachysandra even under pine trees, though the accumulation of needles looks nicer there. I am not thinking of dank city shade in sunless areas between houses. However, English ivy, periwinkle, pachysandra, or that lawn curse, creeping Charlie (or Jenny or money-wort, *Lysimachia nummularia*) will make a satisfactory green covering almost anywhere. Except for Charlie, I don't consider the other three evergreen groundcovers anything but a delight. (However, more anon in Chapter 12 on groundcovers, a big rewarding subject.)

On the east and south, shade tempers the heat. The four trunked balm-tree unfurls sticky aromatic leaf buds in spring in an area of forsythia and dogwood, all underplanted with pachysandra. Ash and sweetgum on the right are pruned high to intercept the strong rays of the sun but still let in enough light for grass to grow beneath their branches. I love the long cool shadows cast by trees on a hot afternoon.

Edge of Shade. If you want flowers, it is important to provide some small open areas that reach beyond the shade into the sun. Although this place is mainly shaded, I have been careful to provide enough sunshine for such annuals as petunias, browallia, and impatiens, and to plant peonies, and some of the finer varieties of day-lilies along the north side of the drive, where they get a few hours of morning sun.

Comfort and Convenience. The comfort of a shaded place cannot be overestimated. One government bulletin states, "You can't alter the weather, but you can allow for it . . . It is said that properly placed shade trees can reduce summer room temperature of a frame house in an arid climate by as much as 20 degrees. This can be translated into dollars if you are paying for air conditioning." Visitors often inquire if my house is air-conditioned and I'm happy to assure them it isn't—only shaded.

To our comfort, shade adds another lovely dimension—shadows. I love the look of the long dark silhouette of the trees on the lawn. On warm summer afternoons, I agree with James Kelly that "Summer is a seemly time," which it is out of the sun and in the shade.

In winter, the sun rises above the east hill. When the leaves are gone and the steep incline is snow-covered, the handsome silhouettes of the trees are seen in bas relief. Viewed from the house through the pair of lawnside crab apples beyond fence and open meadow, the low Sargent crab apple stands in relief and the tall juniper is a dark sentinel beside the bench. Krieg photo.

TALL DECIDUOUS TREES FOR SHADE AND BEAUTY

NAME	HEIGHT IN FEET	GROWTH	SHAPE	REMARKS
Acer, rubrum Maple, Red or Swamp	100	Fast	Irregularly rounded; rather shallow-rooted.	Native, worth planting for conspicuous red flowers; small dark leaves, first to turn red and gold in fall. (Norway maple not so desirable, green leaves have *late* yellow color, less effective, terrible surface roots.)
saccharum Sugar Maple	100	Slow to moderate	Oval to round top; fairly deep-rooted; myrtle thrives under mine.	Native, eastern North America; yellow, orange, scarlet fall coloring is the glory of New England.
Ash, see *Fraxinus* Balm-of-Gilead, see *Populus* Beech, see *Fagus* Buttonwood, see *Platanus*				
Fagus grandiflora Beech, American	80	Moderate	Upright, taller than wide.	Both require considerable space; both with gray bark, darker on European; handsome in every season; leaves turning pure gold in autumn; among finest ornamental; my grove with attendant saplings a great joy. 'Atropunicea' is called the copper or purple beech; 'Pendula' is the weeping beech; 'Laciniata', the cutleaf European.
sylvatica European	80	Moderate	Spreading, almost as broad as tall; let branches reach to ground; roots come close to soil surface.	
False-Acacia, see *Robinia*				

Fraxinus pennsylvanica lanceolata Green Ash	60	Fast	Irregularly oval.	Native, lovely on my lawn. Plant pyramidal 'Marshall's Seedless' to avoid seed nuisance.
Gleditsia triacanthus Honeylocust	125	Fast	High and open, light ferny shade.	Native, good for almost immediate effect. Select the thornless 'Inermis', 'Moraine', or 'Sunburst', with golden young leaves as if in bloom.
Honeylocust, see *Gleditsia* Larch, see *Larix*				
Larix decidua European Larch	100	Fast	Pyramidal in youth, spreading in age as branches droop.	Choice deciduous cone-bearer; a golden flame of needles in autumn before they drop; I prize this.
laricina American Larch or Tamarack	60	Fast	Pyramidal.	Notable hardiness even across northern Canada; common in New England marshy places; not so handsome as European.
Linden, see *Tilia*				
Liquidambar styraciflua Sweetgum	100	Moderate	Rounded.	Eastern native; star-shaped leaves, glorious red-gold autumn color; globular spiny fruits for Christmas decorations.
Liriodendron tulipifera Tulip-tree	100	Fast, long-lived	Cylindrical; pale green and yellow tulip-shaped flowers, June.	Native. Transplant with earth ball while small; big handsome dark leaves, yellow fall color; thrives beside my brook.

TALL DECIDUOUS TREES FOR SHADE AND BEAUTY (*Continued*)

NAME	HEIGHT IN FEET	GROWTH	SHAPE	REMARKS
Locust, see *Robinia* Maple, see *Acer* Oak, see *Quercus* Plane-tree, see *Platanus*				
Platanus occidentalis American Plane-tree or American Sycamore	120	Very fast	High open, lives for centuries; tolerates drought but often drops leaves in midsummer; not for refined lawn area.	Eastern native, volunteered at a distance on brook bank; gray-brown white peeling bark; fruits borne singly; handsome from a distance. Best in moist soil.
X *acerifolia* London	100	Fast	Spreading.	Smaller, more tailored than American plane-tree, holds leaves through summer, ball-like fruits in clusters of 2 or more. Same interesting bark as American plane but more susceptible to caterpillar skeletonizing.
Poplar, see *Populus*				
Populus candicans Poplar, Balm-of-Gilead	70	Fast	This is also called balsam poplar.	Confused with *P. tacamahaca*. If unfurling foliage smells of balsam, it's probably that tree.
tacamahaca balsamifera Balsam Poplar	70	Fast	Tall trunks may grow in clusters of four, as here; handsome form; big leaves but surface-spreading roots reach to 30 feet here.	Not for shade but much admired here at edge of lawn; pulled suckers soon become trees; aromatic spring scent of unfolding leaves pervasive and delightful.
Quercus alba White Oak	100	Slow	Rounded, spreading, a noble tree.	Native, volunteered here on top of cliff when an acorn probably dropped into a soil-filled crack; dark purplish-red in fall.

palustris Pin Oak	80	Moderate	Pyramidal, low branches drooping to ground; fine specimen.	Native, brilliant red in fall, must be pruned high for a lawn tree.
rubra Red Oak	75	Fast	Rounded, spreading.	Native, dark red fall foliage, not for a small area.
Robinia pseudoacacia Black Locust or False Acacia	75	Fast	Upright, straggly in age but picturesque.	Native, valued for jonquil fragrance of pendent flower clusters like short wisteria blooms. Try to find room for it. See also *Gleditsia triacanthus*, Honeylocust.
Salix babylonica Weeping Willow	30–50	Fast	Gracefully pendulous.	Not for planting near the house; surface roots travel far, interfere with drains; offers a lovely contrasting texture and form; mine grows beside the brook.
caprea French Pussy Willow	25			Fragrant for late March; nice to force indoors.
Sassafras albida Sassafras	60	Fast	Rounded, thrives in poor soil, weed tree here, suckers easily.	Eastern native; good for quick shade; beloved of children for "mitten" leaves and aromatic chewable stems; yellow spring flowers, scarlet fall foliage.
Sweetgum, see *Liquidambar* Sycamore, see *Platanus* Tamarack, see *Larix*				
Tilia cordata Littleleaf Linden	50	Slow	Rounded, dense shade; scented blooms June–July but not till 15 years old.	Small, heart-shaped leaves give nice texture effect to this European tree; littering trees not for next the house.
Tulip-tree, see *Liriodendron* Willow, see *Salix*				

In June the silken fringetree is more than a tree; it is a fragrant experience, scenting the house for two weeks, shading the guest room through summer. To the left, the Christmas-berry rises in front of the plant room, letting sun through to the houseplants in winter but protecting them from the hot southern glare in summer. Miner photo.

3. *SMALLER TREES FOR THE PLANTED PLACE*

Flowers and Fruit Come with These

If your place is not too big, say 60 by 100 feet, you will have space for two or three of the smaller trees, those that grow to about 25 feet; if it is larger, you can have many. In any case, select wisely. These smaller trees grow in size and beauty with the years, and the flowering types can take the place of the more demanding perennials you probably used to plant lavishly. I can never have enough of the less mighty trees and I have used them freely, even invading the meadow that I had originally meant to keep for a parking area.

White Birches

Clumps of the native white birch, which properly is called the gray birch, *Betula populifolia,* rise everywhere I look. I think no other tree gives me so much pleasure. Do select yours personally in a nursery. I had to search for the right four-pronged specimen to plant as a sentinel at the front walk, now a lovely tree for me to dwell on from the kitchen casements. From the path I can reach it with a broom to brush the snow from its supple branches, and in winter the night light at the back door shines beautifully upon it. The white-barked clump is always surprising me with a new attraction. One winter morning of deep snow the long catkins showered the ground with a heavy golden dust. When the juncos discovered this bonanza, the birds and I breakfasted together in mutual appreciation of our birch tree. In summer, the leaves rustle coolly with the slightest breeze; in autumn they become triangles of pure gold.

This birch is but one of a number of three- and four-pronged white clumps here. I have planted them repeatedly like a keynote chord in a musical composition. Some are associated with hemlocks, azaleas, and ferns for a composition enjoyed winter and summer beyond the picture window of the plant room. Others stand alone as accent for the entrance to the Round Garden, to the Fern Garden, the foot-bridge and mailbox path, and across the brook with a foreground of rocks and water. Each is a joy to behold—and in every season.

Witch-hazel, Dogwoods, Crab Apples

The early witch-hazel, *Hamamelis vernalis,* rises to 9 feet beside a bench in the Round Garden. In this protected setting, it blooms ahead of spring, sometimes in late February. Casting its sweet fragrance on the mild winter air, it invites me to come and admire the golden flowers. Branches cut for an indoor bouquet scent a whole room.

The other smaller trees of my choice, all producing showy flowers and in sequence, make this place colorful from spring into summer. The Cornelian-cherry, *Cornus mas,* is not so spectacular as many other favorites but I value it because it blooms in most years early in March. This doesn't look like the familiar dogwood with its showy white brachts, but you know it is a dogwood when you examine the small golden fluffs of bloom, which resemble those on *Cornus florida.*

A flowering tree too little known is the Japanese dogwood, *C. kousa.* I have planted it beside the mailbox path, and I enjoy the gleam of its white pointed petals when I pass there on June mornings, for it blooms almost a month after *C. florida.* On the same walk by the bridge, I admire much earlier the spicebush, *Lindera benzoin,* with its spring veil of pale yellow bloom before the leaves appear. It is a native that came uninvited but is most welcome.

The star magnolia, white and glistening, opens scented, silken petals in April at the edge of the driveway, a delight to those who come and go and also to those who stay.

A May treasure, the great silverbell, heavily pruned, arches above the Look-Into Garden where annuals bloom in the sunlight on the open side. Fitch photo.

The familiar dogwoods are trees with never an unbeautiful or uninteresting season from the "tilting planes of bloom" through lush summer foliage to red autumn fruits and handsome winter silhouettes. I prefer the whites to the pinks, which do not seem to blend as well with my landscape. On one white dogwood I let branches droop to the ground where well-fed grass grows underneath. The natural habit of growth of this dogwood gives a different effect than that of any other tree or shrub. Pruned high, another makes a nice small shade tree.

Two 15-foot, pink, early May-blooming crab apples—their varietal names lost in the mist of records—accent the long vista from the house up the back hill. Far across the fence and in the meadow, a Sargent crab apple, more shrub than tree, is a lacy white vision viewed from the house between the pink trees. At the left of the drive, a tall crab apple, perhaps *Malus floribunda,* the Japanese flowering crab, offers fragrant, double, rose-colored blossoms, a great bouquet of color that becomes a bounty of red August-to-mid-October fruits much favored by squirrels and birds. Today catalogues offer a fine selection of crab apples, with white, pink-to-red, single or double blooms, the trees growing from 8 to 50 feet.

At the edge of the Look-Into Garden (described in Chapter 8) the silverbell or snowdrop-tree, *Halesia carolina,* is hung with white blossoms from late April well into May. My tree grows to 25 feet with spreading branches pruned into an umbrella and four-winged pale green seedpods that adorn the tree in summer like another crop of flowers. In the meadow I have planted *H. monticola;* the two trees there are growing fast toward their taller possibilities. These are the only species hardy north, and both offer their pendent flowers before the leaves appear.

Fringetree, Christmas-berry, Hawthorns

It is the fringetree at the front door which is more than a tree, it is an experience. Dripping with silken white panicles early in June, it scents the whole house for two weeks—a beautiful sight, indeed, and a companion for purple lilacs close by. In bloom, the fringetree requires me to sweep the front stoop at least twice a day and for at least a month after blooming while stems and seeds and general debris are cast down. This I willingly do. If you would avoid the nuisance of the fringetree and enjoy only its scented beauty, plant it somewhat beyond your doorway but still in the near view. When the front of the house was knocked out for the plant room, it was suggested that this fringetree or "at least one trunk of it" should be removed so the walk could be exactly centered. I ignored such heresy; the walk was laid off-center, and my treasured fringetree was saved to delight us all with its sweet scent and handsome gray form. I like this tree so much I planted a second one beside the seat in the Round Garden where, following the yellow early spring witch-hazel, it brings fragrance to another area. Be sure to select yours in bloom in a nursery where you can check it for fragrance; I am told some fringetrees have no scent.

The Christmas-berry, *Photinia villosa,* which stands outside the plant room, is deciduous, thus affording the houseplants a full season

In the right meadow, beyond the post-and-rail fence, two silverbells grown there as bushes not trees accent a vista from windows on the east side of the house. Fitch photo.

of sun and then the necessary protection from summer glare and heat. A deciduous tree placed so, next a sunny south window, is a great convenience. This shapely, 15-foot grower, dotted with small white May flowers, is a favorite with nesting robins and other birds that strip off the fall fruits, for which it is named, almost before I see them. Certainly fruits never cling till Christmas. In autumn, after most other trees have dropped their leaves, the photinia foliage turns rosy-amber and glows when the sun shines through.

Beside the terrace the double-trunked white hawthorn, the English May-tree, *Crataegus oxyacantha,* rises to the second story and makes a beautiful canopy seen from my bedroom above. The fragrant, flat, snow-white spring blossoms are followed by bright red fruits, which the birds gradually remove until only three or four clusters hang into late winter, and then one day I will see a hungry nuthatch or a brilliant red cardinal detaching the final one. A ceramic, hanging in the tree, is home to wrens or black-capped chickadees every year. From the porch it is fun to see them building their nests and feeding their young but, watch as I will, I never manage to catch the exit flight of the little ones.

The cream-white Washington hawthorn, *C. phaenopyrum,* puts on an autumn show of scarlet berries that makes you think it's covered with bloom. If you have space, do plant this, but keep in mind that the spread, like that of the English hawthorn, is considerable, to 15 feet or more.

A little beyond the house in the somewhat light shade that is desirable, the elegant goldenchain-tree, *Laburnum* X *watereri* (*vossii*), in mid-May pins on yellow racemes that look like wisteria panicles. If planted with a lavender wisteria vine, the effect is enchanting, but my tree stands somewhat aloof in the little opening at the lawn's edge with hemlocks and more white birches at the side. In this climate there are so few yellow-flowering trees that I particularly cherish this one and only wish the house had more windows so that this tree too could be in closer view.

I should also like to have a few more of these medium-sized trees, especially the European or mountain-ash, *Sorbus aucuparia,* that I admire on my daughter's lawn. This grows to 40 feet and bears white flowers in early summer followed by clusters of brilliant orange-red fruit, much of which clings, despite the robins, until early winter. But enough is enough and an overplanted place may be interesting but it is bound to lack serenity and charm.

SMALLER TREES FOR THE PLANTED PLACE

NAME	HEIGHT IN FEET	FLOWERS, FRUITS FOLIAGE	CULTURE	REMARKS
Amelanchier canadensis Shadbush or Serviceberry	40	Single white April–May flowers before leaves; red berries in early summer soon stripped by birds.	Sun and moist soil; plant away from junipers.	Fine native; yellow to red fall foliage is spectacular; also gray bark in winter; in hot spring weeks, flowering may be brief.
Bechtel Crab Apple, see *Malus* Benzoin, see *Lindera*				
Betula populifolia Gray Birch (but called White)	25	Leaves turn to pure gold early in fall; common through Northeast.	Endures poor or rocky soils; here not so short-lived as claimed, but requires protection from leafminer.	Lovely, graceful, white-barked accents to mark paths or contrast with hemlocks; select three- or four-pronged clumps; choice landscape tree.
Cercis canadensis Eastern Redbud	30	Purple-pink flowers April into May before leaves; brilliant yellow autumn foliage.	Sun or high shade; growth flat at top.	Native New England to Florida, same range as white dogwood, the two are good garden companions.
Chionanthus virginicus Fringetree	25	Silken white panicles in June; last to leaf out; marvelously fragrant; good with multiple trunks.	Sun and good drainage; can be pruned to suit site.	Utterly beautiful, much too little planted; lovely close to house but not just next walk or porch because of much shedding.

Christmas-berry, see *Photinia* Cornelian-cherry, see *Cornus*				
Cornus florida Flowering Dogwood	25	Large flat white or pink blooms in May; shiny red berries late summer to fall; crimson autumn foliage.	Shifting sun; needs deep watering in drought.	Horizontal growth; let branches sweep ground or prune high for a small shade tree. Handsome in every season.
kousa Japanese Dogwood	20	White June blooms, red berrylike fruits, crimson fall foliage.	Sun or open shade.	Bushy growth, nice extender of dogwood season.
mas Cornelian-cherry	15	Small, fluffy yellow blooms in March; red fall fruits.	Naturally spreading but here pruned narrow and upright.	Treasured for dependable earliness.
Crataegus oxyacantha English Hawthorn or May-tree	15	Fragrant, flat, snow-white blooms in May; red autumn fruits that hang into winter; shapely form; thorny.	Sun or light shade; fast-growing.	Don't plant the thorny hawthorns near junipers, allow each a 15-foot spread. Grow as a rounded, low-branched tree or prune high and open to see through.
phaenopyrum Washington Hawthorn	25	Clusters of mid-June cream-white flowers; fine red fruits, scarlet autumn coloring.		Native from Virginia to Alabama; heavy fruiting looks like a second blooming and fruit clings into winter.

SMALLER TREES FOR THE PLANTED PLACE *(Continued)*

NAME	HEIGHT IN FEET	FLOWERS, FRUITS FOLIAGE	CULTURE	REMARKS
Dogwood, see *Cornus* English Hawthorn, see *Crataegus* Fringetree, see *Chionanthus* Goldenchain-tree, see *Laburnum* Gray Birch, see *Betula* Great Silverbell, see *Halesia*				
Halesia carolina Silverbell or Snowdrop-tree	25	White bells, strung along branches late April into May ahead of leaves.	Both halesias good in sun or semi-shade in acid soil.	Here pruned high to umbrella shape; interesting seeds.
monticola Great Silverbell	40	Golden autumn coloring, nutlike fruits; large flowers.		Can be grown with multiple trunks, as in the meadow.
Hamamelis vernalis Vernal Witch-hazel	10	Fragrant yellow ribbon blooms; February or March, upright.	Both natives grow in poor lightly shaded woodland but handsome in full sun in the garden.	Fine for the beginning or end of the growing season; too little planted; choice.
virginiana Common Witch-hazel	15	Spidery, very sweet-scented yellow flowers in late October after leaves fall, vase-shaped.		

Japanese Cherry, see *Prunus* Japanese Crab Apple, see *Malus* Japanese Dogwood, see *Cornus*				
Laburnum X *watereri* (*vossii*) Goldenchain-tree	25	Yellow flowers hanging in clusters, like wisteria, in mid-May.	Light shade.	Be sure to water this one in drought. Fine for early yellow, rare color among flowering trees.
Lindera benzoin Benzoin or Spicebush	15	Tiny, pale yellow fragrant flowers in April ahead of leaves; golden fall foliage, red berries on pistillate or female plants.	Choice plant for damp woodland.	Eastern native, beautiful volunteer here in the woods beside the bridge; crushed leaves are aromatic.
Magnolia soulangiana Saucer Magnolia	20	White to purple-pink, April–May flowers; starts to bloom at 2 to 3 feet; no fall coloring.	Sun or light shade.	Best to transplant magnolias in spring; spectacular trees, need plenty of room.
stellata Star Magnolia	10	White or pink, fragrant ribbony stars March–April before leaves; twisted fall seedpods.	Sun, acid soil here.	Not reliably hardy here; petals turn brown in some springs but worth chancing I think. Sometimes better shrub than tree, as in my Look-Into Garden.
Malus baccata Siberian Crab Apple	40	White, fragrant early May bloom; red and yellow fruits favorite of birds.	Crab apples thrive in full sun in average soil.	Early, extremely hardy. Crab apples native and Oriental among most spectacular garden trees. See Wayside Garden's catalogue for pictures of fine cultivars. The pyramidal 'Columnaris' good for small places.

SMALLER TREES FOR THE PLANTED PLACE (*Continued*)

NAME	HEIGHT IN FEET	FLOWERS, FRUITS FOLIAGE	CULTURE	REMARKS
'Dolgo'	15	White flowers, far-reaching violet scent early May.		Very hardy. Bloom only in alternate years; red fruits spectacular, good for jelly.
floribunda Japanese Crab Apple	30	Pink, early May bloom.		Late August to mid-October yellow and red fruits.
ioensis "Plena" Bechtel Crab Apple	25	Double pink flowers late May. 'Dorothea' modern substitute.		Native; avoid near junipers because of susceptibility to rust. Spectacular green fruits.
sargentii Sargent Crab Apple	8	Small, white, mid-May flowers cover tree for a lacy effect; red fruits.		Japanese native, lowest-growing crab apple, can be used as a single-trunked shrub if given room to spread to 12 feet or so.
May-tree, see *Crataegus* Mountain-ash, see *Sorbus*				
Photinia villosa Christmas-berry	15	Small white May flowers in flat clusters; red fruits favored by birds; great favorite here.	Sun.	Sun shining through clear amber autumn foliage a lovely sight on this shapely grower; choice small tree.
Prunus sargentii Japanese Cherry	30	Deep pink April–May bloom; scarlet fall foliage.	Sun; rich, well-drained soil; needs room to spread.	Upright 'Columnaris' good for small properties; water well in drought. Many other fine cultivars, upright and weeping.

Sargent Crab Apple, see *Malus* Saucer Magnolia, see *Magnolia* Serviceberry, see *Amelanchier* Shadbush, see *Amelanchier* Siberian Crab Apple, see *Malus* Silverbell-tree, see *Halesia* Snowdrop-tree, see *Halesia*				
Sorbus aucuparia Mountain-ash or Rowan	30	Clusters of white flowers in June.	Sun or light shade.	Fine yellow-to-red autumn coloring; brilliant orange-red fruit, much of which clings, despite robins, until early winter.
Spicebush, see *Lindera* Star Magnolia, see *Magnolia* Redbud, see *Cercis* Rowan, see *Sorbus* Vernal Witch-hazel, see *Hamamelis* Washington Hawthorn, see *Crataegus* Witch-hazel, see *Hamamelis*				

In a small area at the corner of the house, the dwarf Swiss stone pine, *Pinus cembra* 'Nana', for five years has taken the place of *Ilex crenata* that quickly outgrew the site. Soil is retained here by an edging board painted dark green; pachysandra is thinned at times to make way for hyacinths and the clematis vines trained up beside the windows.

4. EVERGREENS—THE TALL AND THE SHORT OF THEM

Firm Thoughts on Foundation Plantings

Indispensable for the planted place are evergreens. They strengthen design and make beautiful winter pictures. They also absorb sound; a deep dense evergreen planting here provides a barrier against thruway noise a half mile away. Forest giants, like hemlocks and pines, make fine specimens, hedges, and screens. A line of self-sown junipers makes an interesting silhouette along the brow of the hill. The smaller yews are nice next the house but let's avoid the stereotyped "foundation planting." Broadleaf evergreens—azaleas, mountain-laurels, rhododendrons, and hollies—are to me wonders of nature, and I can never have enough of them. Their foliage is an excellent foil for the needle plants, and the flowers of the first three and the fruits of the hollies are among the most spectacular of all. Rhododendrons make good background plants for a border of hybrid azaleas.

Forest Giants

How you plant the giant evergreens is a matter of preference. If you have plenty of land, you may set them out here and there as specimens, allowing each one an area 20 feet square. Where this is possible, the natural beauty of each one is emphasized; the pendulous, horizontal, or upward sweep of branches, the charm of the cones, upright candles on the various firs, decorative pendents on the pine. The winter effect of a mature, uncrowded specimen is indeed majestic.

I have never planted the big evergreens in this way, being unwilling to afford them so much of the space I have. However, I have enjoyed several associations of a single tree, as a hemlock, with white birches, azaleas, and ferns. For screening the work area of the place—compost heaps and the like—I planted a group of white pines; I set a colony of hemlocks in front of the wall along the street to reduce traffic noise and shield the place from public view; pines and hemlocks inside the post-and-rail fence on the south act as a neighborly screen. American holly, a fine pistillate or female plant, makes a tall accent among low-growing mountain-laurels. A small staminate or male holly, a pleasing evergreen though nonfruiting of course, grows inconspicuously nearby.

The speed at which these evergreens grow never ceases to amaze me. Set out about ten years ago in a 4-foot size, they have quickly reached some 25 feet and are so thick you can't see through them. But I suppose ten years isn't really quick. However, it is surprising what small specimens well cared for will do for you, not to mention the wealth of needles the pines supply for mulching. About fifteen years ago, I planted a larch in the meadow; it's now 30 feet tall. If you do not know the common larch, I urge you to discover its unique beauty of soft glaucous deciduous needles that turn to pure gold in fall. But never plant it in low or wet ground.

Some of the larger evergreens, as arborvitae and hemlock, are good for sheared hedges, also the upright yews, which are elegant and much more expensive. But I wouldn't think of planting here anything that had to be sheared regularly. What a job, and you have to keep up the tailoring once you've started. Instead of a hedge of any kind, I like a fence, since zoning laws permit, and inside this, irregular plantings of tall evergreens or shrubs that don't need spraying or pruning or thinning or mulching every time I glance their way.

Smaller Needle Types

The smaller needle evergreens are extremely useful. I particularly like the Japanese yews. A pair of dwarf *Taxus cuspidata*—'Densa' I think they are—accents the ends of the plant-room window and one of them reaches round to the front steps. These yews are cut back late in spring or early in summer to keep them shapely and in scale. At Christmas more trimming is in order to supply holiday greens. If plants get a too-thick bunched look, I reach low into them with my loppers and cut out a few not-too-thick old growths. With these I allow a 6-foot width but am stern on height above the present 3 feet. In general, yews are slow-growing and thrive in sun or shade. They do best in cool, moist soil. Choose the variety according to your purpose: for under windows, beside doorways, at the angle of a building, for hedges. Heights vary from 1 foot to 50 feet.

The Hatfield yew is broadly columnar and can be used at the corners of house or garage. It doesn't require much basal room. Hicks yew is narrowly columnar, and makes an attractive, low, clipped hedge, should you want such; it is also good for a narrow bed between house and walk. You don't have to let it grow to its full 6 feet.

Junipers come in all sizes and shapes from creepers to trees. Watch out for path plantings of Pfitzer. Even if you set this back from the line, it will probably widen so you'll have to keep shearing, and then it's difficult to avoid an unsightly, one-sided growth. The Canaert upright juniper, like the Hatfield yew, can serve as a corner planting. Avoid the Hetz juniper in foundation plantings; it grows 15 feet tall and spreads as wide. The various creeping junipers make superb groundcover, some growing only 10 inches high. Let's think about them in Chapter 12.

The globe arborvitae of formal appearance is a plant I just don't want. To me it looks artificial. Unfortunately, it is much used in foundation plantings where it sometimes is allowed to grow 12 to 15 feet tall. When it is kept low by flat shearing, I think it is a sight. It's a pity to plant this when so many other evergreens will stay low naturally.

How Firm Is Your Foundation Planting?

The idea that every foot of house foundation must be concealed as soon as construction is finished is one of the banes of suburbia. Since my own concept of next-to-house plantings runs, as I describe in Chapter 13, to little dooryard gardens and specimen shrubs or groupings with the accent on fragrance, there was little here to photograph as a model. On that account, looking for attractive plantings elsewhere, one day I drove up and down the streets of this town where small houses are set on small lots and large dwellings on the required two acres or more. And what did I find—old overgrown plantings of unsuitable evergreens, some concealing not only first-floor but often second-floor windows as well. I saw desperate rhododendrons struggling, *unmulched,* in full sun. Even new plantings did not suggest appropriate futures, for they were thickly planted to include, it appeared, some of everything the nurseryman had on hand or the owner admired. And shade trees dotted about the new lawns instead of opposite, and not too far from, the windows they were to shade, made me shudder for the in-and-out mowing job they would necessitate.

Perhaps excuse can be made for foundation plantings made twenty years or more ago. There was not then available in the trade the number of slow-growing and dwarf conifers and broadleaf shrubs we have today. But there is also no doubt that few owners gave thought to the growth potential of, say, a pair of arborvitae or cryptomerias at a front door or upright yews under windows. Even with *careful* yearly pruning these cannot be kept small enough for such locations so plants must either be butchered to size or allowed to grow unchecked with the house cowering behind them. Complete removal and replacement by more suitable material is really the only answer.

At *your* doorway, instead of the Oriental arborvitae species with its 60-foot possibilities, consider the dwarf Alberta spruce, *Picea glauca* 'Conica'. You can see very small specimens in the urns beside my doorway. Under your windows, a low-growing *dwarf* Japanese yew like *Taxus cuspidata* 'Densa' would be attractive—and satisfactory. In a quarter of a century, it will hardly reach 4 feet though it will spread wide. A little judicious pruning will keep these chunky plants shapely without formalizing them.

Dwarf and slow-growing plants are necessarily more expensive than the fast ones since the nurseryman's profit also grows slowly, but in the end these less exuberant evergreens not only save you money and upkeep but guarantee you a continuously good effect at the front of your house. Incidentally, don't set evergreens, or for

This simple foundation planting complements the long lines of a clapboard cottage. A pair of slow-growing dwarf Wilson rhododendrons (*R.* X *laetevirens*) on each side of the entrance steps, a specimen of Japanese pieris at the corner, and graceful curving beds of pachysandra make an attractive undemanding evergreen planting that sets off but does not conceal the building.

A grouping of interesting plants grows by this front door. The climbing hydrangea clings to the brick chimney with white-flowering dwarf azaleas accenting the steps, and a leucothoe behind them. At the corner, concealing the garage entrance, is a tall rhododendron.

This is an example *not* to follow. The small house cowers behind tall fast-growing arborvitae that dwarf it and cut off light and air from the windows. The mammoth ill-chosen Japanese yews look awkward and require a great deal of pruning to hold them even to this unsuitable height. The cure here would be to dig out and throw out, replacing with dwarf or slow-growing evergreens that would decorate not desecrate. The idea that every foot of foundation must be concealed by evergreens is a bane of suburbia.

that matter any plants, under the eaves where no rain ever falls. Instead, spread a 12-inch or wider strip of gravel or stones to discourage weeds in that unreachable area, and put your plants in front, well before it.

Slow Growers and Dwarfs

I hope knowledge of the slow growers and the dwarfs won't come as late to you as it did to me. In fact, it took me several years to recognize the fact that however pretty a small specimen of Japanese holly, *Ilex crenata,* looked in the 4-foot area at the corner of my house, it could not be contained there long. After two years, I moved it to the driveway bed, where it now grows, with mild pruning, 6 feet high and 5 feet across. And then I did it again. Traveling fast through a local nursery in spring, anxious to fill the vacancy, I again planted a *small* attractive Japanese holly. Of necessity transplanted, this one in a proper location, has now grown 4 feet high and 4 feet across.

A specimen of the charming Swiss Stone pine, *Pinus cembra* 'Nana' now graces the corner. After five years, it is only 40 inches high and some 15 inches across. I salute its self-control every time I pass. Another favorite of mine is the slow-growing *Pinus mugo* 'Compacta' or Swiss Mountain pine, rounded and spreading, and so easy to keep to 3 feet, well below its 5-foot possibility. It's a handsome dark green and dense grower of interesting habit.

Other slow-growing evergreens and also the dwarfs are worth investigating. Now that properties are smaller today, the smaller plants look in better scale with them. There are also midget evergreens. In eight years my tiny *Pinus mugo pumilio* has grown almost not at all and it makes a pleasant prickly accent for the end of a walk.

A number of nurseries today specialize in dwarf forms of pine, spruce, hemlock, and others. I list some growers in "Where to Buy." Perhaps a local nurseryman can supply you. As you walk through the rows of plants, check the botanical names. Look for 'Compacta', 'Nana', 'Pygmaea', 'Minima', obvious indications of reduced size; *repens* and *procumbens* proclaim low spreaders. If the plants you want are not available locally, your nurseryman can order for you or you yourself can send to a mail-order firm that specializes in dwarf evergreens. To visualize what you will be getting, look at the big specimens for type and shape and then picture them small.

The dwarf *Ilex crenata* 'Hitzi', a compact Japanese holly that does not require clipping, is an excellent evergreen to plant under windows.

The small-leaf evergreen, *Cotoneaster microphylla,* is the just-right ornamental for difficult places, as this corner area along a brick walk. It won't exceed 3 feet and can be used as a specimen. Scarlet fall berries are a colorful dividend.

Broadleaf Evergreens

In this classification are some of the most beautiful—and useful—material on this planted place. The small-leaf, compact, low-growing varieties of *Ilex crenata* like 'Helleri' and 'Stokes' that hardly reach 3 feet are excellent for planting near the house. Real dwarfs also occur among the ilexes: 'Kingsville Green Cushion' hardly reaches 10 inches and has less than a yard spread; 'Mariesii' is only 6 inches high. These smaller broadleafs are excellent for northern or western locations with acid soil.

For foundation plantings in the sun, you may want to avoid rhododendrons as I do. Too often, if they survive at all, they live in obvious despair. This is usually because they have not been properly mulched and deeply watered. Furthermore, only a few are suited to situations in full sun, as the Carolina hybrids—'Ramapo', 'Purple Gem', 'Windbeam', 'Wyanokie', and the P.J.M. hybrids. The dwarf Wilson rhododendron will also take sun. However, I have another reason for not enjoying rhododendrons on close view in winter. I don't like the way they roll up their leaves in cold weather. They look as if they were freezing to death and they make me shiver, even though I know they are only reducing leaf surface to conserve moisture. I am told that mine is a feminine reaction and that men like to check temperature by the leaf curl of rhododendrons. In fact, someone has observed that the Carolina gives the first signal and rolls up at 20 degrees. I find rhododendrons much more satisfactory planted away from the house in a border protected from wind with low azaleas in the foreground.

If you plant one of the evergreen barberries under your window or along the front walk, you won't have to shear or prune much. Threespine barberry grows only to about 3 feet and warty barberry may not exceed 2 feet. Littleleaf Korean boxwood is another small, under-3-foot evergreen welcome near the front door. However, it does not have the gloss of the English boxwood, which may grow to 20 feet and serve elsewhere in your plantings.

These evergreens, grown for foliage not bloom, are included in the chart of Choice Broadleaf Evergreens following Chapter 5. Rhododendrons (azaleas are kinds of rhododendron), mountain-laurel, leucothoe, and many other broadleafs produce flowers of great beauty. These also are considered with other flowering shrubs in Chapter 5.

Evergreens for special uses. *Above: left,* a Norway spruce, *Picea abies clanbrassiliana,* that won't reach 6 feet for years and years; *right,* the familiar Andorra creeping juniper 'Plumosa' that won't grow above 18 inches but will eventually spread over a 6-foot area. *Below:* left, for a narrow border Wilson rhododendron edged with dwarf boxwood; *right,* the Swiss Mountain pine, *Pinus mugo* 'Compacta'.

TALL EVERGREENS FOR SPECIMENS OR SCREENING

NAME	HEIGHT	GROWTH	SHAPE	REMARKS
Abies concolor White or Colorado Fir	75	Medium	Dense and pyramidal, finely textured, blue-green needles.	Rocky Mountain native; good specimen where room; upright tapered cones; don't prune off lower branches, not renewable.
Arborvitae, see *Thuja* Cedar, see *Juniperus* or *Cedrus*				
Cedrus atlantica glauca Atlas Cedar	120	Fast	Widely pyramidal, silvery, light-green effect.	Develops a flat top with age; not the same as the pointed red-cedar, *Juniperus virginiana*, which see. Does well near the sea.
Chamaecyparis obtusa Hinoki False-cypress	80	Slow	Broadly pyramidal, dark and glossy.	Excellent specimen for a big place, also good for screening.
Cryptomeria japonica Cryptomeria	125	Fast	Irregularly pyramidal with tiny rounded cones.	Individual, elegant, for formal rather than country places; develops enormous girth; a tree I like to dwell upon, though it browns somewhat in winter; requires protection from sun and wind.
False-cypress, see *Chamaecyparis* Fir, see *Abies* Hemlock, see *Tsuga*				
Juniperus virginiana Eastern Red-cedar	80	Fast	Columnar.	Native, transplant with ball; lives forever, native on top of my sunny back hill and in New England meadows.

Picea abies Norway Spruce	90	Fast	Upright spreader with pendent branches.	Cones hang down, good specimen. Not the blue spruce, *P. pungens*, that hardly ever looks right anywhere.
Pine, see *Pinus*				
Pinus nigra Austrian Pine	80	Rapid	Pyramidal, may have flat top in age, stiff dark needles.	Strong and handsome as a specimen, for mass screening or formal hedge. Plant all pines in full sun.
strobus Eastern White Pine	125	Fast	Tall, broad pyramid; finely textured; branches good for summer fireplace bouquet or winter arrangements.	Native with large cones; transplants easily; good screen from neighbors or to hide compost and trash piles. I depend and dote on it. Lovely in all seasons.
Spruce, see *Picea*				
Thuja occidentalis American Arborvitae	60	Fast	Pyramidal to round; flat fanlike sprays; can be clipped as a hedge.	Giant native, too often used in foundation planting, needs water in heat and drought; often browns in winter; mentioned for you to avoid; I don't like it.
Tsuga canadensis Canadian Hemlock	90	Fast	Shapely, graceful pyramid, feathery, long-lived; can be clipped as a hedge.	Native, among loveliest of evergreens, fine as specimen or screening; I combine with white pines along boundary fence; 'Pendula' the Sargent hemlock, flat on top, seldom higher than 4 feet but up to 50 feet across. Hemlocks tolerate shade as pines do not.

NEEDLE EVERGREENS FOR SMALL PLACES

NAME	HEIGHT IN FEET	SPREAD IN FEET	CULTURE	REMARKS
Juniperus chinensis 'Pfitzeriana' Spreading Juniper	5	Spreading 6 to 12 feet, fast-growing.	Sun, tolerates poor soil, even drought.	Junipers among hardiest of evergreens; pfitzer feathery and arching; small-growing Compact Pfitzer useful.
c. 'Sargentii'	1	8 to 10.		Fine gray-green groundcover.
horizontalis 'Douglasii' Waukegan juniper	1	Low, trailing branches.		Steel-blue cast toward purple in winter.
h. 'Emerson'	1	Very slow-growing.		Prostrate, blue.
h. 'Plumosa' Andorra juniper	1½	Low, ascending branches, spreading to 6 feet or more.		Prune regularly to avoid legginess and let light into lowest branches. Bronze in fall; more compact than Waukegan.
procumbens Japanese Garden Juniper	2	Low and spreading.		Bluish green needles not so vigorous as *J. horizontalis* 'Nana'; excellent rounded dwarf form.
sabina tamariscifolia Tamarix Juniper	4	Fast-growing, spreading and mounded.		Feathery light green; endures city pollution, considered "best variety."
virginiana Eastern Red-cedar	50	Narrow to widely pyramidal.		Slow-growing species, attractive.
v. 'Canaertii'	12			Dense rich green. Showy bluish fruits.
Picea abies Norway Spruce		Compact pyramidal form.	Endures heat and drought.	Smaller cultivars many uses; fast-growing.

a. 'Procumbens'	3	To 15.		Prostrate horizontal branches.
a. 'Pumila'	1	To 6.		Dense, flat-topped.
a. 'Repens'	2	To 5.		Arching, procumbent.
glauca "Conica" Dwarf White Spruce	8	Compact pyramidal form.		
Pinus cembra 'Nana' Swiss Stone Pine	3	Tightly pyramidal.	Sun, tolerates wind.	Hardy, very slow-growing, foliage same color as white pine.
mugo 'Compacta' Mugo or Swiss Mountain Pine	4	Rounded.		Hardy, grows slowly when young, good for doorways, foundations, needs some pruning to keep small and shapely.
m. pumilio	½	Tiny and spreading.		A bristling cushion.
Taxus baccata 'Repandens'	4	Nearly prostrate; leaves blue-green. Flat-topped with pendulous branch tips.	All yews thrive in sun or shade, even north side of house.	Hardiest of English varieties, and fruiting.
cuspidata 'Densa' Dwarf Japanese Yew	Can be kept below 4.	15 or more.		Very hardy. Try to select female plants with attractive red berries.
c. 'Nana'	5	4 to 5.		Judicious pruning keeps it low; no shearing necessary.
media 'Hatfieldii' Hatfield Yew	10	Broad columnar.		For corners of house, not beside front door.
m. 'Hicksii' Hicks Yew	6	Narrow columnar.		Excellent for hedge.

Outside the plant-room window a pair of *Viburnum carlesii,* trained as vines, bring color and scent to the front door late in May. The slow Christmas-berry has not yet leafed out; the yews below are pruned to space.

5. *FLOWERING SHRUBS, DECIDUOUS AND EVERGREEN*

Beautiful Means to Little-Work Gardening

The flowering shrubs—deciduous like the lilac, broadleaf evergreen like the mountain-laurel—can be the beautiful mainstay of your planted place. Well chosen, they provide a glorious panorama of spring-to-frost bloom, grand house bouquets, interesting fruits and berries, and green beauty through the cold months. The broadleafs can be counted on to strengthen the landscape effect; deciduous shrubs alone may have a thin look. With the two groups you can plan winter as well as summer pictures to enjoy from the various windows of your home.

A simple, satisfactory planting for a small place consists of shrub borders, straight or curved and as wide as possible, with pockets for hardy bulbs and a few reliable perennials. Plan such borders along the outer edges of your yard around a center lawn section—small enough to hand-tend if you want fine grass. Or the center can be a pebble area, particularly suitable if yours is a house of contemporary design. Plant one of the smaller flowering trees on the lawn and prune it high to give you shade, or let your lawn—or pebble area—

stand free to the sun while you enjoy comfortable coolness on an adjacent porch. If you edge the shrub border with brick for a tidy look without clipping (one wheel of the lawn mower runs over the brick), mulch the plants deeply, and interplant the maturing bulbs with bought-in-bud annuals, you will have as colorful and carefree a garden as Nature ever permits.

If you don't actually know many shrubs, maybe only forsythia or mock-orange for sure, do see what the many other available shrubs look like. Get a copy of the Wayside Gardens (Mentor, Ohio, 44060) spring catalogue. It costs $2.00 and is well worth it for all the plants are illustrated in color.

Around Stony Brook Cottage, I have planted a number of azaleas, winter honeysuckles, lilacs, mock-oranges, and viburnums. Under the dining-room windows, which face west, is a bed that could, I suppose, be termed a foundation planting. Here a pleasing association of flowering broadleafs includes the 6-foot Japanese andromeda, *Pieris japonica,* at the corner of the house, its *drooping* braids of bloom white and fragrant late in April. In May the tufted chartreuse flowers of the Oregon holly-grape, *Mahonia aquifolium*—neither holly nor grape—open to be followed in summer by clusters of blue berries. These hardy plants grow to 4 feet here. In June that treasure among broadleafs, the mountain-laurel, *Kalmia latifolia,* is covered with pink-white shell-like flowers. It could grow very tall but is easy to keep low and broad below the 4-foot window ledge. Royal ferns fill out this bed that is hedged with clipped blue periwinkle.

Along the sheltered northern boundary fence, where I can look down upon them from my study, the 4-foot mountain-andromeda, *Pieris floribunda,* with clusters pointing up, and drooping leucothoe, *L. catesbaei,* mingle with low-growing rhododendrons, but these broadleafs do not bloom so well here in the shade as elsewhere in shifting sunlight. I also planted the Japanese skimmia; though this latitude is somewhat north of its preference, still it thrives.

I bought the rhododendrons in beautiful lavender bloom but every year since planting the buds blast in the cold. It's a good idea to keep in mind when spring enthusiasm envelops you that nurserymen are aware of your condition then and some may offer plants of doubtful hardiness because they can be brought up from the South in full bloom and are therefore immediately salable. In any case, I think rhododendrons with or without flowers are excellent broadleafs especially for the back of borders with perhaps lower shrubs in front.

In mid-May the lovely Carolina rhododendron—it's supposed to be the first to roll its leaves at 20 degrees F—opens rosy purple blooms on plants unlikely to go above 5 feet.

The Lovely Azaleas

As for the azaleas, deciduous and evergreen, who can have a garden without them? They are listed as rhododendrons by botanists and some nurserymen, for azaleas exhibit only minor differences, if any, from other rhododendrons. Many of the loveliest ones are indigenous to our own Eastern woodlands from Florida to Maine. All produce spring-into-summer flowers, many with a fine clove scent, and to this a few add the glory of brilliant autumn foliage. They require an acid humusy soil, cool moisture, and protection from wind. They will tolerate some morning sun but prefer light shade or shifting sunlight under tall oaks or open pines. I mulch the shallow roots with pine needles or decaying oak leaves. They cannot endure drought or extreme heat. Bark sold in bags also makes a good mulch.

Of the deciduous species the first to bloom, in April, is the pinxterbloom, *Rhododendron nudiflorum* of our New England woods, often known as wild-honeysuckle. Its flowers are pale pink to nearly white.

Closely related to it and close on its heels is *R. roseum,* the roseshell azalea, with pink to pale crimson fragrant flowers with pink stamens. It is hardy as far as Quebec. Both species bloom before their leaves develop.

Also early is *R. mucronulatum,* profusely covered with rosy-lavender to rosy-violet flowers, a variety of a Chinese azalea and effective with forsythia. By mid-May the Royal azalea, *R. schlippenbachii,* begins to open its masses of 3½-inch-wide clear pink fragrant flowers.

A new Exbury Hybrid azalea, 'Golden Peace', brings more of this favorite hue to my green hemlock and laurel groupings. The flowers are large, to 6 inches across, with a spicy fragrance; the plant is well branched; and the foliage a lovely red-bronze shade in fall. Courtesy Conard-Pyle Co.

The semi-evergreen bayberry, *Myrica pensylvanica,* whose berries have been used for candles since colonial days, grows here beside a seaside cottage; in my garden, in fairly deep shade, it makes a fine specimen clump.

It is one of the best, brought from Korea eighty years ago. Also at this season another American species, the tall pinkshell azalea, *A. vaseyi,* puts forth its superb light-pink flowers. The American flame azalea, *R. calendulaceum,* is an orange-flowered species of great beauty for early June. It is native from Pennsylvania southward but hardy in southern New England and much of New York. The clove-scented flowers vary from pale to dark tones, have long exserted stamens, and are well set off against dark leaves.

By this time the many handsome deciduous or semi-evergreen hybrid azaleas are conspicuous in my friends' gardens. It was long my discipline to avoid the lovely cultivars because I had sense enough to know they would really capture me—and now they have. Three years ago I visited the Oliver Nurseries near me in Fairfield, Connecticut, when those hybrids were at their height of bloom—and I *was* lost. Now every spring I find space for a few more. The Gable, Glenn Dale, and Kurume strains are not dependably evergreen everywhere; they may be semi-evergreen or perform as handsome deciduous shrubs with colorful fall foliage. The ones that particularly please me are the double salmon-pink 'Louise Gable' and 'Ruth May', the dusty-pink 'Aphrodite', the fine whites 'Palestrina' and

'Delaware Valley White'. This last one shines out from the Cliff Walk, a striking picture from across the brook.

Various other hybrids are a glory here from April to June in the Fern Garden and elsewhere, especially the golden 'Nancy Waterer', and yellow-touched white 'Toucan', and the very fragrant cream-white 'Daviesi' also with yellow markings. Although this place is in Zone 6 on the U.S.D.A. *Plant Hardiness Map,* and some azaleas are not recommended for planting north of Zone 7, all these thrive here. I have lost only one plant, a Mollis hybrid, the exquisite yellow 'Directeur Moerlands', but I am replacing it for a second trial. However, it may fail again, for the Mollis hybrids sometimes find our summers too hot. In any case, I suggest you let your local nurseryman advise you, but be adventurous. The new 'Golden Peace' azalea from Conard-Pyle sounds irresistible. It is described as spicily fragrant and a bright deep yellow.

In mid-June as the pageant of the hybrids ends, the 10-foot smooth azalea, *R. arborescens,* casts its sweetness beside the brook and at the back of the Fern Garden, the pure white clusters accented with rosy filaments. Finally the 12-foot swamp azalea, *R. viscosum,* produces small but richly clove-scented white flowers with white filaments. It grows naturally in wooded swamps from Maine to South Carolina, particularly near the coast. For me it blooms in late June–early July, in a happy company of hemlock, white birch, mountain-laurel, and fern.

Winter into Spring

It's the very early flowering shrubs that mean so much to me. I literally smell spring when, toward the end of February or early March, the winter honeysuckle opens its tiny, powerfully fragrant blossoms. This shrub is choice; set at the southeast corner of the house, it scents the whole area clear to the kitchen, which is 30 feet away. It is almost evergreen, holding its green ovals far into January. I prune it to an open, 8-foot fountain instead of permitting its naturally straggly 15 feet. I never see this anywhere else; I don't know why it is so neglected, for I can't recommend it too strongly.

Forsythia, usually considered the spring opener, actually doesn't color until late April, although branches can be cut and forced in the house in February. The showy border type, *F. spectabilis,* grows to 10 feet or so and is most welcome. I like it here as a specimen—

Four beautiful flowering shrubs. *Above: left,* the evergreen rose daphne, pink and very fragrant in mid-May, sometimes again in December, is worth some effort; *right,* the franklinia, here just ready to open its kid-glove cups, blooms August to frost in the Look-Into Garden. *Below: left,* early in spring in the evergreen border that starts at the steps of the brook, the mountain-andromeda, *Pieris floribunda,* opens white upright clusters on an evergreen plant 4 feet high, though 6 feet is its goal; *right,* the Japanese dogwood, *Cornus kousa,* with pointed "petals" blooms after the familiar *C. florida.*

well pruned it has a handsome vase form in winter—or set on both sides of a driveway so you can drive through its yellow glow. Blooming ahead of leafing, it is enhanced by evergreens, as here with hemlocks. Excellent cultivars include: 'Beatrix Farrand', upright and vivid, and 'Spring Glory', a paler yellow. The weeping forsythia, *F. suspensa,* is lovely on a bank or foaming over fence or wall, and 'Arnold Dwarf', growing to 4 feet, is good for small gardens.

About the same time the golden flowering currant, *Ribes odoratum,* dispenses a clove scent by the fence in the meadow. As showy as forsythia, if given the space it can also grow to 6 feet.

Indispensable Viburnums

The great clan of viburnums includes one very early bird, the March-into-April fragrant guelder, *V. farreri* (*fragrans*). I baby it in a protected southern corner of the house where to date it is nothing to cheer about. However, I am hopeful that those rose-red buds some spring will open into the rich-pink scented blooms I once saw in abundance on a plant in Toronto in the midst of a snowstorm—and fresh and unspoiled afterwards.

At least six other viburnums are cherished here, and I'd gladly plant more, for there are no shrubs more durable, more beautiful, as, for example, *V. carlesii.* This familiar fragrant viburnum pins on its coral brooches late in April and for ten days they scent this place for 50 feet around. I planted it first under a bedroom window so my guests could enjoy the spicy sweetness but it kept aiming at 6 feet with a spread almost as great so I moved it beside the stone fence on the north and let it go its expansive way. Then I set a pair of the same viburnums on each side of the plant-room window facing south. There I am growing them espalier-fashion and they are enchanting, up 7 feet now with little bunches of pink-tinged blooms peering around the corner to the front door.

The fragrant snowball, *V.* X *carlcephalum,* blooms a week after *V. carlesii,* with larger flowers and the same fine carrying scent. It took it two years to get going in the somewhat shaded location that is its lot in the northern boundary with broadleaf evergreens. Now it is reaching toward 8 feet. I put it there with a carpet of blue violets so that I could look directly down upon them both from my study window.

Just across, next the house, is the tea viburnum, *V. setigerum* (*theiferum*). Early in summer it blooms white with a lily scent. Then come clusters of glistening red berries and bronze tones in the leaves.

According to Dr. Donald Wyman, the Japanese snowball, which has evidently suffered an identity crisis, is now called *V. plicatum;* it was formerly *V. tomentosum plicatum* or *V. t. sterile.* This is the familiar one with rounded clusters late in May. At one time its variety, *V. p. tomentosum,* the doublefile viburnum, graced the Look-Into Garden but soon expanded so fast and far in height and girth I had to move it to the entrance end of the driveway. There in a corner of the post-and-rail fence it makes a handsome 8-foot sentinel, the horizontal growth an arresting contrast to mainly pyramidal growers. On the upper surface of the flat branches, showy white flowers open early in June. These are followed in August by red fruits, bright as a second blooming, and colorful autumn foliage. The variety 'Mariesi' is considered the best for fruit but the bloom is likewise outstanding.

The European Cranberry-bush, *V. opulus,* bears red fruit, not very good to smell, and there is an interesting variety, 'Xanthocarpum', with yellow fruits. The red fruit of the familiar American cranberry-bush, *V. trilobum,* is edible, and the form 'Compactum' well suited to the small place. These two species grow to 10 feet.

Lilacs for May

Lilacs belong to New England as magnolias to the South. Lilacs were one of my first considerations here since a colonial house without them is unfinished, and if anyone protests that they are rather straggly growers, it is for me a matter of pistols at dawn. You can select varieties to bloom from April into late June but the last have a smell not a scent. Here May is lilac time. Then bloom the varieties of nostalgic fragrance and endearing beauty.

The common lilac, *Syringa vulgaris,* came in with the colonists. Planted beside the kitchen door, purple or white, it opened in May with the scent of home. Today, hundreds of varieties later, the common lilac, which grows to 20 feet, still gives uncommon pleasure, and I can never pass up the great bouquets of it offered in the market.

However, the hybrids, especially the doubles, are more intensely fragrant and the blooms are larger. Here, when allowed to, the plants grow house-high and give an ancestral look to a cottage little more than twenty years old. Blooming along with the pink crab apples, they make a lovely harmony. Along the south-facing living-room windows, shading them and the western casement of the plant room, are the deep purple 'President Lincoln' and the lighter blue-toned 'President Grevy'. In the Look-Into Garden the dark violet 'Ludwig Spaeth' grows beside the white 'Vestale', both delectable singles. Across the driveway the double white 'Ellen Willmott' does not grow so tall as these other 7- to 9-foot beauties, nor is it so floriferous but every scented white truss is handsome.

There are pink lilacs, too, like 'Esther Staley' and 'James McFarlane' and a so-called yellow, the creamy 'Primrose', but for me the range of lavender to deep purple and the whites suffices. Mine are all tall growers. For a small garden, an under-5-foot specimen or two would be more suitable like the rounded purple *Syringa palibiniana* (*S. velutina*) 'Miss Kim', or the two-toned, daphne lilac *S. microphylla* 'Superba', which blooms in June and sometimes again in August. In time, I will plant more of the tall French hybrids now that I no longer need the meadow for parking. Among whites there are three very fragrant doubles: 'Mme. Lemoine', 'Mme. Casimir Perier', a creamy color, and the ivory-tinted 'Edith Cavell'. I should like also the lavender 'Victor Lemoine' and the richly fragrant, deep violet 'Cavour'. Indeed, I wish for too many lilacs as for too many other fine shrubs, so excellent are many of the plants in this category.

It is sometimes claimed that lilacs take a couple of years to get going and then bloom well only every other year. This has not been my experience but I take care to water plants well in drought and to feed them heavily. Unlike most of my other shrubs, these must have sweet soil and will not thrive in acidity. It is a good idea to work lime liberally into most soils before planting and in generally acid soils to top-dress each spring with lime. I also apply wood ashes from the fireplace for potash, and superphosphate in spring to promote bloom.

With the hybrids, take care to remove any suckers rising from privet roots if plants are grafted, and occasionally prune out at the base some of the old, nonbearing wood, especially in the center. Cutting off faded clusters keeps your bushes looking neat but it is not essential. True, seed formation takes away some nourishment but my plants bloom well despite many pods left at the top, those I cannot very well reach. If your lilacs grow so tall and leggy that you can't see the bloom, you may want to do a serious renewal job and

Espaliered against a white clapboard house, this well-trained firethorn (*Pyracantha*) blooms white in May and sets a spectacular crop of long-lasting orange berries late in summer. Yews and an *Ilex crenata* make pleasing doorway accents.

cut off much of the growth at the base. Then the plants will hardly be things of beauty for a couple of years but will be forced to produce new flowering branches lower down. It's wise not to let plants get so out of hand you have to do this but instead to reduce some of the tall growth each year.

Mock-Oranges for June

Also called syringa, the mock-oranges are properly *Philadelphus*, and a very fragrant tribe. The European *P. coronarius* is the familiar, old 9-foot shrub with scented bloom from late May well into June. Victor Lemoine used this in developing his handsome, large-flowered hybrids, but not all are so richly perfumed. I have the tremendous 9-foot spreading 'Virginal' not quite so scented as the species but very pleasing, though it gets leggy with age. It thrives now beyond the fence where space is no object. 'Innocence' to 8 feet is a prolific bloomer with single flowers; it is considered one of the most fragrant of all. 'Belle Etoile' is a very fragrant hybrid, graceful and arching to 5 feet, and almost as broad, with cerise touches at the center of the flowers; it blooms a little later, mid-June into July, and longer than the two-week flowering of most mock-oranges. I have also liked 'Avalanche' for smaller quarters since it grows only to 4 feet, likewise 'Mont Blanc', the single blooms of both being well scented. However, if fragrance is important to you, as it is to me, try to select in-bloom mock-oranges, and lilacs too, in the nursery. There can be a great difference in plants, even of the same species or variety. I have had arguments about the fringetree, mine being so scented it fills the house, while others report no perfume at all, and I wonder if we are discussing the same tree.

In *The Fragrant Year,* the book in which Léonie Bell and I describe our many fragrant favorites, we have this to say about the time that scents are strongest:

"When is the fragrance of flowers most noticeable? We observe that the hours of strongest scent are not the same, even for the same plants. It depends on the essential oils, which are present in varying amounts at different times of day and night; they evaporate at different speeds and at different temperatures. Most roses smell sweetest on a mild damp morning as the sun strikes them, reach a crescendo at noon, and may be scentless by night. The same flowers may pour out a stronger perfume in a protected corner than in the open, and exposure to sun, as well as to weather, affects them. Drought and heat often rob flowers of sweetness, and flower scents vary slightly from youth to age."

The shrub classification is so vast, I have not even mentioned all of those I grow here, as the butterfly-bush, *Buddleia davidii,* or *Spiraea* X *vanhouttei* now in uncramped quarters across the fence, and the shrub althea, or *Hibiscus syriacus* along the drive. There too grows a handsome, 6-foot specimen of the wild blue huckleberry, *Gaylussacia,* with gorgeous autumn color. It is hardy and deciduous, *G. frondosa,* I think it is; certainly it deserves recognition. My landscape architect, Margaret Baillie, pitying the early bareness of this place had several dug up from her fields and planted here for me. The bayberry shrub, a *Myrica* species, now 6 feet high and as wide came the same way. After twenty years, I am still grateful for them both.

CHOICE BROADLEAF EVERGREENS FOR YEAR-ROUND EFFECT

NAME	HEIGHT IN FEET	FOLIAGE, FLOWERS, FRUIT	CULTURE	REMARKS
Azalea, see *Rhododendron*				
Berberis julianae Wintergreen Barberry	5	Yellow flowers, blue-black fruit.	Sun.	Barberries make good spiny hedge plants that need no trimming.
X *mentorensis*	3	Inconspicuous May bloom, dull red fruits.		Semi-evergreen, stands more heat and drought than most.
triacanthophora Threespine Barberry	3	Blue-black fruits.		Evergreen, very thorny.
verruculosa Warty Barberry	2	Dark purplish fruit, shiny leathery leaves.		One of the best of the evergreen barberries; bronzy autumn foliage.
Buxus microphylla koreana Littleleaf Boxwood	2	Excellent foliage.	Shade.	Useful for low hedge; hardier than English. Avoid winter wind as leaves may brown. See newer cultivars as 'Tide Hill' or 'Wintergreen'.
sempervirens Common Boxwood	20			Marvelous, shining hedge or accent plant, slow-growing, may be sheared or not.
suffruticosa Dwarf Boxwood	6 inches			Fine for edging.
Cotoneaster dammeri Cranberry Cotoneaster	1	Red fruits on long branches.	Sun or shade.	Larger fruits and a better plant than the familiar rockspray, *C. horizontales*, which is a scrawly thing here.
Daphne cneorum Garland or Rose Daphne	½	Very fragrant, pink flowers mid-May, sometimes to December.	Needs winter protection, cool moist roots, loose *sweet* soil.	Evergreen, difficult but worth effort, called the "drop-dead plant" by some, so unexpectedly does it disappear.

CHOICE BROADLEAF EVERGREENS FOR YEAR-ROUND EFFECT *(Continued)*

NAME	HEIGHT IN FEET	FOLIAGE, FLOWERS, FRUIT	CULTURE	REMARKS
Ilex crenata Japanese holly 'Helleri' 'Stokes'	5–10	Beautiful small-leaved mounded growth.	Sun or light shade.	Species excellent, fast-growing, undemanding, nice for doorways or with small flowering trees as here along driveway; can be pruned to 5 feet; cultivars, dwarf and compact to 4 feet.
Kalmia latifolia Mountain-laurel	15	June, pink-white shell-like flowers, also deeper pink to red cloves.	Sun or semishade.	Easy to keep low by pruning; one of the very best.
Leucothoe catesbaei Drooping Leucothoe	3	April–May.	Stands heavy shade here.	Small graceful shrub, good in association here with andromeda and mountain-laurel.
Mahonia aquifolium Oregon Grape-holly	4	May, fragrant chartreuse flowers; blue summer fruits.	Sun or part shade.	Can be rampant, traveling far by underground runners, stands hard pruning.
Pieris floribunda Mountain Andromeda *japonica* Japanese Andromeda	6 9	Upright, white pyramidal clusters. Mid-April, drooping fragrant flowers, just before *P. floribunda*	Semishade.	Hardy, fine for on-view plantings out of the sun.

Pyracantha coccinea lalandi Laland Firethorn	8	White flowers in large clusters in May; in fall, spectacular orange berries.	Sun.	Attractive against a wall or tied to a trellis.
Rhododendron—Azalea Gable, Glenn Dale, Kurume Hybrids	5–10	April to June, pink, white, yellow, orange, red.	High shade of oaks or open pines; acid humus soil; protection from wind; supply mulch.	These may prove evergreen; it depends on location and weather. Try to select in-bloom plants in a nursery.
Rhododendron catawbiense Catawba Rhododendron	8	Mid-June, white, pink, red, big spreading plant.		Natives; good for northern locations; allow 6 feet for most.
carolinianum Carolina Rhododendron	5	White to purple.		Some hybrid varieties will stand, even prefer, considerable sun, and more than this species.
maximum Rosebay	12	Pink to white, June.		This one makes a 12-foot spread.
R. X *laetevirens* Wilson Rhododendron	3–4	Early June, inconspicuous pink.	Part shade.	Dense, billowy, slow, pruning unnecessary.
Skimmia japonica Japanese Skimmia	2	White spring blooms, then red fruit.	Part shade.	Male and female plants both necessary for bloom; needs sheltered location to survive this far north. Small size makes it useful.

SOME FAVORITE FLOWERING SHRUBS

NAME	HEIGHT IN FEET	BLOOM	CULTURE	REMARKS
Abeliophyllum distichum White Forsythia	5 and mounding	Mid-April with a honey scent before leaves.	Sun or semishade, tolerates alkalinity.	Hardy and easy though flower buds not always weatherproof except in a protected location.
grandiflora Glossy Abelia	5 and as wide	Pink-white, June–August.		Not the greatest but useful for its habit of long blooming.
Buddleia davidii Butterfly-bush	12	July–August, fragrant spikes of white, pink, red, purple.	Cut to ground in spring, renews like a perennial.	Attracts butterflies; 'White Bouquet' and pink 'Charming' are good cultivars.
Calycanthus floridus Sweet-shrub	5	April–June, brown-purple flowers, leaves, and bark all aromatic.	Sun or semishade, undemanding.	Hardly ornamental but delights children; cut pieces to force indoors to scent winter rooms.
Chaenomeles japonica (*Cydonia*) Flowering Quince	1½–6	May, before shiny leaves, white, pink, red, orange.	Sun.	Makes a strong prickly hedge; or low specimen, nice to work into foundation areas.
Clethra alnifolia Summersweet, Sweet Pepperbush	9	Fragrant white spikes of blooms, July and August.	Native, for moist soil and high shade.	Fine carrying scent.
Daphne burkwoodii 'Somerset'	4	Cream-white to pink flowers in May; red fruits.	Light shade.	Vigorous and free-blooming evergreen.
mezereum February Daphne	3	Far-reaching fragrance; late March.	High shade, sometimes naturalizes.	Easy and revels in cold. Magenta or white flowers; scarlet berries in June, evergreen.

Deutzia gracilis Deutzia	2 to 3	May, white flowers.	Sun or semishade.	Good for front of border planting.
Forsythia spectabilis and Varieties Goldenbells	10, arching growth in sun or shade	Late April–May before leaves.	Sun, light shade, easy.	Fast-growing, endures city conditions, handsome as specimen or good for tall unpruned boundary plantings; also dwarf and weeping forms.
Franklinia alatamaha	6	White flowers, August to frost.	Sun or open shade.	Prized for its late blooming; a tree to 30 feet in the South.
Gaylussacia frondosa Wild Blue Huckleberry	6	Tiny, bell-shaped greenish flowers; edible fruits.	Shade, acid soil.	Fine fall coloring, as attractive as many cultivated shrubs.
Hibiscus syriacus Shrub Althea or Rose-of-Sharon	5	Summer to fall; white, pink, purple, variegated.	Sun or light shade, trouble-free.	Many cultivars, not distinguished, singles best; endures city and seashore. Useful for midseason color.
Kerria japonica Kerria	5 and as wide	Bright yellow, May through summer.	Heat and drought resistant.	'Pleniflora' is double; I prefer single form.
Lonicera fragrantissima Winter Honeysuckle	6 and as wide	Late February–April; tiny, piercingly sweet fragrant flowers before leaves.	Sun, semishade, easy even on north side of house.	Choice; leaves hold well into January; can be pruned to arching form.
Myrica pensylvanica Bayberry	6 and as wide	Aromatic foliage, gray waxen berries.	Tolerates poor, sandy soils.	Semi-evergreen. Berries used to make fragrant candles.

SOME FAVORITE FLOWERING SHRUBS (*Continued*)

NAME	HEIGHT IN FEET	BLOOM	CULTURE	REMARKS
Philadelphus coronarius Mock-orange	9	Late May–June, white scented flowers.	Sun, semishade, no trouble.	Prune all of them after bloom to keep stocky, not thin at base.
Varieties	4–8	Singles and doubles, June–July.		Try to select in-bloom plants to check for fragrance. Small growers and big ones where plenty of space.
Potentilla fruticosa Buttercup-shrub or Gold-drop	3	Golden June–October flowers and fine-cut leaves.	Very hardy and sun-loving.	Good in front of border or with evergreen background beside house; useful, not outstanding.
Rhododendron—Azalea Species and Hybrids	3–12	April–June, white, pink, rose, yellow, scarlet.	Acid humusy soil; cool moisture, mulch, wind protection, light shade or shifting sunlight.	Species excellent for open woodland, some very tall; small hybrids for important placement. Rhododendrons all evergreen, also some azaleas.
Ribes odoratum Clove-currant	6	Mid-April; charming companion to forsythia.	Sun.	Branches force well in winter. Alternate host of the white pine blister rust but no problem here.
Salix discolor Pussy Willow	20	Late February–March, silvery catkins.	Sun, semishade, will soon take hold from short branches stuck into brook bank.	Native in Eastern North America; fast-growing; the French pussy willow of the florist is *S. caprea*.
Spiraea prunifolia Bridalwreath	9	Mid-May, button blooms.	Sun or shade, no problem.	Red-orange autumn color pleasing, not spectacular.
X *vanhouttei*	5	Late May, flat white clusters.		Arching growth, showy, excellent foliage.

Syringa microphylla 'Superba' Daphne Lilac	5	June, sometimes again in August; two-tone pink to lavender.	Sweet soil; plenty of water and fer tlizer.	Indispensable, fragrant, for big and little gardens; plant as many as you have space for. French hybrids are the important ones.
palibiniana Dwarf Korean Lilac	3–5	May, purple, rounded dwarf type.		
vulgaris Common Lilac and French Hybrids	7–20	May, lavender, purple, pink, white.		
Viburnum carlcephalum Fragrant Snowball	8	White flowers in May, fine carrying scent.	Sun, semishade, average soil (acid here), undemanding once established.	Birds like the fruit. Large blooms, fine plant.
carlesii Pink Snowball	6 and as wide	Late April–May coral blooms, very fragrant.		Blooms only for 10 days but absolutely essential; nice to espalier.
farreri (*fragrans*) Fragrant Guelder	10	March–April, pink, scented.	Needs protection, buds may winterkill.	An early one to try but not depend upon.
opulus European Cranberry-bush	10	Red fruits.		'Compactum', good flowers and fruit for small garden.
plicatum tomentosum Doublefile Viburnum	8 and as wide	Late May, flat flowers on flat branches; brilliant red fruits in August.		Horizontal growth, effective contrast to pyramidal growers needs a lot of room; superb 'Mariesii' best fruiting form.
setigerum (*theiferum*) Tea Viburnum	10	June, small fragrant flowers, then red fruits.		Bronze fall foliage.
tribolum American Cranberry-bush	10	Edible red fruit.		Red fall foliage, 'Compactum', small form.

Along the gray stone wall the early Virginia bluebells, *Mertensia,* bloom and multiply in a border of blue forget-me-nots, lavender Jacob's-ladder, and ferns. Mertensia dies down soon after blooming but its brief appearance is enchanting.

6. "PERFECT" PERENNIALS FOR THE PLANTED PLACE

Colorful Spring, Summer, and Autumn Accents

The handsome plants we call perennials, because they come up year after year from hardy roots, are almost too attractive. How often in the past I have succumbed to their lure beyond strength and sense. But today I do not find a wide and lengthy flower border necessary to my happiness—quite the contrary. Instead I want perennials as accents in front of shrubs, in clumps beside a step or in the corner of the house where a little color goes a long decorative way. Of course I want, too, as I imagine you do, one or two small bright mass plantings like my Apple-Tree Garden or the Look-Into Garden near the kitchen door, both judiciously furnished with the least bothersome perennials.

Today I want only "perfect" perennials. And my first criterion of perfection is not bloom; first is good foliage—except for two spring indispensables, bleedinghearts and Virginia bluebells. In others I tolerate no shabby weeks. I require good looks from spring emergence until autumn departure, for fine green leaves make a planted place attractive even if there isn't a flower in sight, and I have found

The perennial white astilbe 'Deutschland' is used here as an accent shrub beside steps made of pebbles. Too-little-known, the white, pink, or red astilbes, growing 18 inches to 4 feet, are reliable plants with strong ferny foliage. Blooming from June to August in light, in some places here in quite deep, shade they associate well with day lilies and are not afflicted by either pest or disease.

any number of perennials that fill this bill. I select certain irises and peonies for spring; mainly daylilies for summer; for fall, the hardy asters, called Michaelmas daisies, and *potted* chrysanthemums; for winter into spring, the Christmas roses.

My second criterion is inherent good health, no phlox with mildew, no plants with pest appeal, as bearded iris to borers, and a generally amenable disposition, as drought tolerance in daisy types. Otherwise, spray gun or duster becomes a constant companion with staking an exacting side issue, as for giant delphiniums.

Thirdly, as the preacher says, I want a lot of flowers from each perennial, great bursts of bloom for at least three weeks, as from peonies and daylilies, or the long continuance not too sparse that Chinese delphiniums and species columbine provide. And I require edging plants never to lose their looks but to be reliable in foliage and flower, as hardy candytuft, coralbells, and clove pinks. (See also the Voice of Experience on edging plants.)

In return for perfect perennials I, alas, will not engage to be the perfect gardener. But there is a minimum that all my plants *can* count on! I will always set them out in well-prepared soil. I will allow adequate room in a location of their preference for sun or shade. I will give one thorough clean-up cultivation in spring, working in the remains of last year's mulch along with a generous application of a complete fertilizer. Finally I will spread more mulch. When they are in bud and bloom or there is a period of drought, I will water them deeply. But that's it, except of course, for the pleasant pastime of snipping off faded flowers, but bouquet-gathering takes care of most of that. Here then are some of the perennials to which the term "perfect" can be applied as I have defined it.

Spring Accents—Irises and Peonies

Bold clumps of the lance-leaved irises offer fine foliage contrast to shrubs or the rounded clumps of peonies and the fountains of day-lilies. In the past I have enjoyed a sequence with the beardeds, *Iris germanica,* that brought vivid color for a full month, from mid-May to mid-June. Today, guided by the pleasure principle, I no longer grow plants with problems that I can't prevent with good sanitation, and borers on the beardeds are one. However, their beauty is undeniable and they may seem to you worth the trouble. In case you are willing to cope, this chart includes a full spectrum of early-to-late varieties of proven excellence.

RECOMMENDED VARIETIES OF TALL BEARDED IRIS

E—early, mid-May; M—midseason, May 21; ML—midseason to late, May 27; L—June on.

VARIETY	COLOR	HEIGHT IN INCHES	SEASON
'Amethyst Flame'	Light violet, ruffled	38	ML
'Blue Baron'	True blue	40	M
'Blue Sapphire'	Silvery, ruffled	40	E
'Captain Gallant'	Copper-red	34	M
'Chinese Coral'	Peach-pink	37	L
'Eleanor's Pride'	Powder blue	38	M
'Fluted Haven'	White, ruffled, robust	35	E-M
'Fuji's Mantle'	Bicolor, white, blue-tinged falls	35	ML
'Heartbreaker'	Glowing pink	36	ML
'Judy Marsonette'	Deep flamingo pink	34	M
'Mary Todd'	Warm red brown	38	ML
'Orange Parade'	Clear hue	38	E-M
'Primrose Drift'	Pale true yellow	42	ML
'Prince Indigo'	Very dark purple	38	L
'Southern Comfort'	Creamy yellow	36	M
'Ultrapoise'	Golden shade	34	ML
'Winter Olympics'	Sparkling white, ruffled	38	E-M
'Zantha'	Large, golden yellow	35	E

Give bearded iris a well-drained location in full sun; if the soil is acid work in lime *before* planting. Steamed bone meal is an excellent fertilizer, about a cupful to a square foot, dusted on and worked in. To plant, prepare a 10-to-12-inch-deep hole for each rhizome, drawing soil up in a mound. Place the rhizome on top of this. Slant the roots down around the mound and firm the soil over them; let the rhizome stay on top with only a sprinkling of soil above it, but be sure the rhizome is well anchored. Give superphosphate in spring about three weeks before flowering and bone meal in late June after blooming. Apply both as side dressing, not *on* plants. Wait till fall to cut back leaves and clean up beds. Green leaves are still full of nourishment.

You can avoid borers on the beardeds by spraying with Malathion —or apply your all-purpose garden dust—as soon as growth appears in spring, again when plants are 6 inches high, and maybe a third

The Christmas-rose, *Helleborus niger,* is a choice evergreen perennial for a permanent location in cool open shade with protection from wind. Usually it is not until late February that it opens in the Look-Into Garden.

time before flower buds show color. (Specialists advise every two weeks!) If you see a punctured or ragged leaf—a sign of borers—cut it off below the point of attack, or squeeze the leaves to squash the invader. Rhizome rot resulting from borers is a hazard requiring root surgery and disinfecting. If all this puts you off—and it certainly does me—skip the beardeds and content yourself with some of the species and the Siberian and Japanese types, none of which has been borer-prone here.

The fluffy white perennial meadowrue with ferny foliage volunteered in the Fern Garden in front of the dark trunks of a wild cherry in a bed of yellow daylilies and ferns. Lovely plants like this 8-foot summer-blooming *Thalictrum polygamum* come of their own accord in woodland plantings, and this is one perennial I willingly stake.

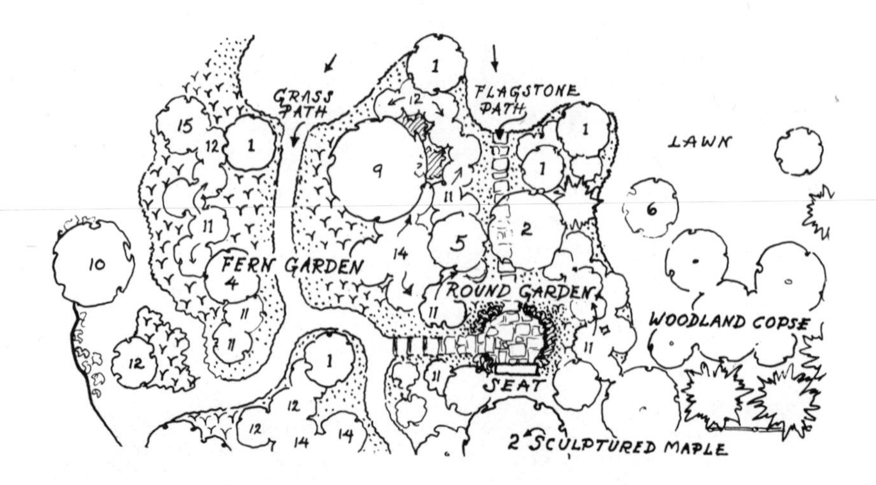

The bulbous gold-flecked *I. reticulata* gives near-winter bloom, late February to mid-March, nice beside a protected doorstep in the sun, and I enjoy patches of the little, crested amethyst spring species, *I. cristata,* and the 12-inch white or darker purple *I. tectorum,* the roof iris of China. Below the plant-room window, these bloom in light shade, sharing space with golden 'Rembrandt' daffodils and the purple-striped white crocus 'Pickwick', but one August also with a nest of yellow jackets, to my painful surprise. For a pocket of something small with good foliage, think of the 8-to-10-inch lavender or white *I. gracilipes,* a darling plant, and maybe you will like the colorful dwarf *I. pumila* with a big head, and a small body, but this looks grotesque to me so I don't plant it.

In June, clumps of the grassy Siberian iris make showy accents in the foreground of a shrub border. I like the clear blue 'Gatineau' with the early yellow daylily *Hemerocallis flava,* the darker 'Caesar's Brother' with white 'Festiva Maxima' peonies, and the pale 'Snowcrest' anywhere. Late in the month the purple *I. versicolor,* which appeared along the brook, blooms there and in the Fern Garden, where I planted it as contrast for the feathery royal ferns.

Through June and July, the elegant Japanese *I. kaempferi*—white, pink, lavender, or purple, the flowers 6 to 10 inches across on stalks 2 to 3 feet high—are striking enough for dramatic placement. These irises like "wet feet, dry ankles," and their roots covered with 2 to 3 inches of humusy, acid soil. Mine flourish at the end of the Fern Walk with astilbes, and across the brook near a great tree trunk with rocks and royal ferns. Japanese iris and pool, pond, or brook are natural associates.

Late in spring the Fern-Garden path, terminated by birches, has a bright binding of purple-and-white woods-hyacinths, mingled with lavender-pink wild geraniums. Behind this colorful edging, ferns elongate and the mounds of daylilies spread to cover the retreat of the bulbs. Fitch photo.

Peonies are handsome from the first rosy April spears, through ferny foliage, to the last frost-touched autumn leaf. And peonies don't need disbudding, nor are those spring ants harmful, so don't worry about them. But do make up your mind about locations, for peonies do not take to a peripatetic life. Some of mine have been blooming well in the same place for more than fifteen years. They get a dose of superphosphate in spring and, for potash, a spread of wood ashes from the fireplace later when I get to it. I thrust wire tripod supports around them at the first sign of spring growth to keep the big plants orderly.

If you are as fond of peonies as I am you may want to emphasize this perennial in your plantings and you can have a fine May-to-June sequence if you plant both the shrubby Japanese and the herbaceous Chinese types.

Sequence of Peony Bloom

May 10–30	Japanese Tree Peonies, *Paeonia suffruticosa* (*moutan*)
May 20–30	Lutea Tree Peonies, *P. suffruticosa* X *lutea*
May 25 on	Early Chinese Peonies, *P. albiflora* (*lactiflora*) hybrids
May 30 on	Midseason Chinese Peonies

After many years my own list of favorites is formidable so I'll just say you'll have satisfaction and pleasure from such old favorites, all double and more or less fragrant, as the white 'Festiva Maxima' and 'Kelway's Glorious', pink 'Myrtle Gentry' and 'Sarah Bernhardt', and red 'Mary Brand' and 'Philippe Rivoire'. Singles like 'Krinkled White' and the deep pink 'Sea Shell' are particularly fine for bouquets.

The usual recommendation is to set out peonies mid-September to early October but I confess I plant—and have moved them—at my convenience in spring, even early summer (then with special care). Obtain well-rooted plants with three to five eyes and set the crowns no more than 2 inches deep in firm loam, no more than 3 inches in very light soil. The pink buds or "eyes," protruding from the roots, should be just below the soil surface. Allow 3 to 5 feet for each plant with sun for at least half the day, and all day is not too much except for the pale pinks, which incline to fade.

When peonies don't bloom it's usually because they have been planted too deep or in shade and competing with tree roots. However, if buds form and then blast, suspect botrytis blight. Cut off buds and burn them in spring and spray with Phaltan or other fungicide. In fall, cut stalks to ground level and burn them.

Oriental poppies will also sparkle for you from late May through June, but I've given them up because they disappear after blooming until new crowns appear late in August. Flowers are handsome but weeks without foliage do not make a plant perfect.

For Summer—Daylilies, Daisies, Some Others

Daylilies, *Hemerocallis,* are *the* summer plants and you hardly need anything else. They are the most dependable of all perennials with handsome endearing foliage and in my experience they are absolutely pest- and disease-free. I grow them everywhere, even in a dim corner where an astounding red one lights up the darkness. If you plant the lemon-lily, *H. flava,* you can have a succession from May 15 to early fall but the glorious effulgence comes in July and early August.

Although each flower does last but a day, and hence the name, the great stalks of daylilies bear so many blossoms that the flowering of a single, well-grown plant is long—beyond four weeks—if kept well watered through budding and blooming. Height variation adds convenience to beauty with dwarfs like the 20-inch fragrant 'Little Cherub', which begins to open in mid-June, to plant at the foot of shrubbery and taller ones like the 36-inch 'Rare China', also fragrant, to set among low shrubs or with a background of evergreens, fence, or house wall.

Some varieties stay open or "extend" their bloom into evening, like the golden 'Jake Russell' and paler yellow 'Chetco'. The "evergreen" group is adapted to the South, the "dormant" or hardy daylilies are for the North, although many of the best in each group thrive in climates where you don't expect them to. I appreciate those green fountains of foliage that look so cool in hot July and are persistently green into December.

Culture is simple. Daylilies require little but space—at least two feet between all but the dwarf varieties, better three feet if you hope to leave plants unattended but uncrowded for four or five years. And the space between is fine for groupings of early narcissus. You can set out daylilies at any time, even in bloom, but late August or early September in the North is most propitious because it gives plants time to establish before cold weather checks growth. And in the North, you will be selecting mainly dormant types.

Daylilies will live and, to a degree, bloom under almost any conditions, but they perform handsomely if allowed at least four hours of sun a day and if they are planted in well-drained, fertile soil. In spring I sprinkle superphosphate around each plant and also wood ashes for potash, as I do with peonies, but you can apply any all-purpose fertilizer high in phosphorus (for flowers). And if there is no heavy rain, do water deeply when plants are producing buds and bloom and also if summer drought occurs.

Take care not to plant daylilies too deep. Set each one with roots well spaced out in a wide hole so that the "crown," or point where roots join foliage, will not be covered by more than 1 to 1½ inches when the soil is filled in and well firmed.

Some 8,000 daylily cultivars are available and the end is not in sight. I must always have the early lemon-lily, *H. flava,* and such old varieties as the richly fragrant midseason 'Hyperion' and 'Kindly Light' with its spidery petals, and 'Colonial Dame', all yellows, and the spectacular pink 'Evelyn Claar' that follows peony bloom along the driveway. I like a few late September ones, too, like golden 'Fidelity', and pale salmon-pink 'Postlude', whose small, hardly spectacular flowers conclude the season. Actually there are few for this time since hybridizers seem to have lost interest in such final-finals.

FINE DAYLILIES FOR TODAY

E—early, mid-June to July; M—midseason, July 1–21; ML—midseason to late, July 21–August 10; L—late, August 10–September.

VARIETY	COLOR	HEIGHT IN INCHES	SEASON
'Annie Welch' Wide-petaled lush blooms	Flesh pink	24	M
'Ava Michelle' Pale with green throat, ruffled, many awards	Yellow	28	ML
'Bess Ross' Best red, vivid, long-blooming	Red	36	M
'Cartwheels' Spectacular flat blooms	Gold	24	M
'Chetco' Round, good sheen	Creamy yellow Evening	32	M
'Curls' Popular miniature	Melon	20	M
'Evelyn Claar'	Salmon-pink	25	E-M
'Emperor's Robe' Large blooms	Orchid-rose	25	E-M
'Fairy Wings' Primrose shade with green throat	Yellow	34	E-M
'Frances Fay' Fine form, wide petals, prolific, many awards	Melon and cream	24	M
'Green Shadows' Greenish shading with dark-green throat, heavy substance, very fragrant	Yellow	30	M
'Irish Heart' Large, pale and flaring with green throat	Pale yellow	34	M
'Jake Russell' Wide, round form, heavy texture	Yellow-gold Evening	34	E

'Little Cherub'	Yellow	20	E
'Luxury Lace' Small, delicate blooms with green throat, many awards	Lavender-pink	24	ML
'Pink Superior' Soft creamy shell pink, small green throat, lovely	Pink	24	M
'Satin Glass' Pale, suffused pink and lavender, famous, "breathtaking"	Greenish-lemon-pink	36	M
'Shooting Star' Pale, rounded bloom, old but holding its own	Yellow	34	ML
'Step Forward' Creamy tone, darker edge, round bloom, ruffled	Pink	30	E-M

Many of the daisy types make good accent plants because they are in flower a long time and gracefully endure summer drought and humidity. The 30-inch yellow anthemis 'Moonlight' blooms from June to October in full sun. The 2-foot modern gaillardias without dark color streaks, 'Sun Gold' and the glowing copper 'Burgundia', make a steady showing through June and July. Either could brighten the edge of a long summer-green shrub border.

The 2-foot Shasta daisies for the same period will give you fine flowers to cut. 'Alaska' is a single white, 'Mark Regal' somewhat taller shows some orange in the center; the glistening, crested double 'Mount Shasta' blooms June to frost. Plant these with your yellow daylilies for pleasing summer pictures. Then there are two lavender daisies, under 2 feet, Stokes aster, 'Blue Star', and the fragrant, shade-tolerant *Aster frikarti* 'Wonder of Staffa', both for July to October. I do like these and, if annual asters have not reciprocated your affection, these two may, their foliage sturdy and orderly, associating well with shrubs.

For mass planting among shrubs rather than foreground accents, there are three transitional daisies to carry summer brilliance into autumn glory. Varieties of Helen's-flower, *Helenium* (this named for Helen of Troy not H.V.P.W.), bloom from July into October. The 4-foot 'Riverton Beauty' and 'Clippersfield Orange' and the 15-inch 'Pumilum Magnificum' (a substitute for coreopsis, being more restricted) will give you baskets of summer flowers. The 4-foot true perennial sunflower, *Helianthus decapetulus,* for July and August gives the effect of a small yellow dahlia. It's a rampant grower to put in a big sunny space where finer things may have failed. The false sunflower, *Heliopsis scabra,* 3 to 4 feet, makes a magnificent August-to-frost display and doesn't run all over like the helianthus. 'Gold-Greenheart' is a pretty variety, nice to cut and good for drying.

You aren't possibly going to want all these carefree daisy-types but just one tall kind among your shrubs, another low one in front of them will give you bright blooms to relieve the summer green.

Three More for Summer

Here I want to say a kind word for the Chinese (Siberian) delphinium, not in it for elegance with the handsome tall hybrids but so much less trouble, no staking, no seasonal doldrums due to heat and disease. If you want blue in your garden all summer long, grow *Delphinium grandiflorum* (*chinense*), the light 'Cambridge Blue' or darker 'Blue Mirror', nice feathery 18-to-24-inch plants. Biennial, but they bloom the first of September from April sowings and the next year buds show at the end of June. Cut plants back after blooming to insure successive crops. I also like the pale 'Belladonna' and darker blue 'Bellamosum', 4-foot perennials that resemble the giant hybrids. The 'Connecticut Yankees' are 2½-foot dwarfs of the Pacific Giants. All of these are manageable delphiniums.

Then there is the too-little-planted astilbe, sometimes erroneously called spirea, blooming from June to August in light shade. A marvelous, ferny-foliaged plant with fragrant steeple blooms of white, pink, or red. The astilbe is, indeed, a perfect perennial. The white 'Deutschland' and pink 'Peach Blossom' are my favorites.

For late summer, August into September, I depend on the self-supporting, dignified *Hosta* (*Funkia*). The foliage is magnificent not only with shrubs but cut and arranged in a green glass bowl for a cool hot-weather effect. With ferns near the house I have the old-fashioned fragrant white, August- or plantain-lily, *H. subcordata grandiflora,* with 2-foot stems.

In a circle inside the laurel bushes in the Round Garden, big glaucous 2-foot plants of *H. sieboldiana* with lavender flowers grow in shade, an effective contrast to the ferns there. And incidentally, this hosta and others make excellent groundcover plants for shady locations.

Because of their spring-to-frost good looks and excellent disposition, these shade-preference hostas are increasing in popularity and more and more varieties are becoming available. *H. minor alba* stays at 12 inches; 'Fortunei Robusta' reaches to 6 feet; others with white or lavender flowers are intermediate in stature.

Autumn—Chrysanthemums and Hardy Asters

To strengthen the holdover color of the summer perennials, I buy some potted chrysanthemums in tight bud in September just to set strategically around the place, only a few being actually planted. I think chrysanthemums are the glory of autumn but roots take up a lot of floor space in my small gardens, and most chrysanthemums need division and resetting every second or third spring, if they are in prominent view, as well as constant pinching back through summer to make them bushy.

I let the growers do this for me now and buy as many of their shapely in-bud potted plants as the exchequer allows. They look lovely placed on top of any empty spaces and are always enjoyed in the dooryard gardens and on the steps. Mine is a lazy procedure but by September I need to be a little lazy. Sometimes I give away the potted plants after bloom to friends who have more time or energy or space for these late bloomers. Set out among bulbs, the late-appearing chrysanthemums hide maturing bulb foliage and a nice two-plant spring and fall association develops. Grown satisfactorily but hardly to perfection, with division not before the third or fourth year—but with regular pinching—the chrysanthemums in this way do a colorful and useful job.

The hardy hybrid asters or Michaelmas daisies—American natives improved by European hybridizers—only find a place in extensive shrub plantings because, again, the tall ones take up long-season room before offering fall color. They must have full sun and plenty of space—crowding causes mildew—and adequate summer moisture. Furthermore, most need staking and, like chrysanthemums, frequent division. But they do make lovely misty clouds of bloom.

The dwarf and semidwarf Oregon asters can be planted for an edging if you don't want early color there. For the center of a border the 24- to 30-inch white 'Alaska', lavender 'Aquilla', and purple 'Archbishop' are pleasing and prove more tractable if only three stems are permitted per plant; these then must be staked with inconspicuous bamboo. The taller asters can be controlled with the wire tripods removed earlier from the peonies.

Winter—the Christmas Roses

My evergreen hellebores or Christmas roses, the last of my perfect perennials, do not always bloom in December, in most years not until late February or early March; it depends on weather. But the flowers last for months, turning from white to pink and at the end looking almost artificial. However, the fat and numerous flower buds can be seen low down in the plants before the late chrysanthemums are spent. I always plant Christmas roses, *Helleborus niger,* in the near view, close to the house where I can enjoy the flowers from a window when cold weather hardly invites distant inspection.

At the start it takes patience with these hellebores. Usually they do not bloom either the first or even the second year after planting, since they must, before setting buds, attain an unusual degree of maturity. Therefore it is important at the outset to select permanent quarters for them. A cool, moist, lightly shaded situation with protection from north and west winds, which tend to burn foliage, seems best. The closer plants are to a protecting wall the earlier they will bloom and their taste for shade makes them a special boon. In a fern bed or at the edge of shrubbery, hellebores will thrive in average garden soil, better still in loam well mixed with leafmold and sand with a top dressing of compost maintained.

Set out plants any time, spring to October, August the most propitious month. Let the roots stretch down, not out, in each 16-inch hole with the crown of the plant just under the soil surface. Good drainage is the great essential; standing water will not be tolerated by the fleshy roots. Summer watering is only necessary if plants wilt, and this may occur in under-tree plantings like mine.

Some new leaves push out in spring; when a plant has reached the 6- or 7-leaf stage, it may be time to divide it. Sometimes the buds on *H. niger,* for example, come up so thickly they can hardly find space in which to open. Even in the first year of flowering there may be half a dozen blooms to a plant. In the course of a decade one specimen will be capable of sufficient division to provide some thirty plants. However, hellebores are generally slow-growing perennials and are better off if divided only for good reason.

The delights of inconsistency are part of the pleasure of hellebores. Cutting fresh flowers in winter, picking basket and shears in hand but boots on the feet for snow protection, is a rare experience. Midsummer blooms grown in the open on midwinter plants—therein lies the charm of the hellebores.

Despite my insistence on perfection, I must have, as I mentioned earlier, two old-fashioned favorites—pink bleedinghearts and Virginia bluebells. Both have good health but bloom only briefly and then disappear totally. Even so, I treasure them.

The other perennials we have been discussing are only a few of the many you could plant given space and energy. In case you don't wish to be so selective as I am, on the following pages are suggestions for many more, some of them also "perfect."

INDEX TO SOME EXCELLENT PERENNIALS

If no information follows entry, refer to the botanical name.

NAME BOTANICAL AND COMMON	HEIGHT IN FEET	COLOR	SEASON	REMARKS
Achillea				
filipendulina 'Coronation Gold'	3	Bright yellow	June–Aug.	Fine for drying large flowers.
ptarmica 'The Pearl'	1½	White	June–Sept.	Carefree; excellent for garden or cutting; ferny foliage; small fluffy blooms, filler for bouquets.
Alyssum saxatile citrinum	1	Pale yellow	Apr.–May	Lovely edging plant.
Anchusa azurea				
Italian Bluegloss				
'Dropmore'	3–5	Deep blue	June–Aug.	Good tall blues for border in full sun.
'Opal'		Pale blue		
Anemone				
japonica	2–3	Pink, white	Sept.–Oct.	Among best for autumn.
pulsatilla	1	Purple	Apr.–May	Enchanting for edging or rock garden.
Aquilegia				
caerulea	2	Lavender	May–June	Dainty, airy plants, Rocky Mountain columbine, partial shade for all of these.
chrysantha	2	Yellow	May–July	Bushy, floriferous species.
McKana Hybrids	2½	Pink, purple, red, yellow, white	May–July	Large, long-spurred blooms.
Artemisia 'Silver King'	3	Gray foliage		Good mist plant for "peacemaking."

Aster, Hardy	½–5	All but yellow	Sept.–Oct.	Essential fall accents, dwarf and giant, lacy effect.
Astilbe, Hybrids	1½–4	White to red	June–Aug.	Shade, marvelous plant, ferny foliage.
August-lily (Plantain-lily), see *Hosta* Babysbreath, see *Gypsophila* Balloonflower, see *Platycodon*				
Baptisia australis	2–3	Blue	June	Foliage and flower good.
Basket-of-gold, see *Alyssum* Bleedingheart, see *Dicentra*				
Brunnera macrophylla (*Anchusa myosotidiflora*)	1	Blue	May–June	Fine true-blue forget-me-not flowers; large spreading. Deep moist soil.
Caltha palustris Cowslip or Marsh-Marigold	1	Yellow flowers, big spreading leaves.	Apr.–May	Fine color in swampy area below Cliff Path.
Candytuft, see *Iberis* Carnation, see *Dianthus caryophyllus* Carolina-lupine, see *Thermopsis*				
Chrysanthemum, Garden *maximum* *parthenium*	1–3 1½ 1½	All but blue White White	Sept.–Dec. June–Nov. June–Oct.	Fall indispensables, cushion and tall. Fine for cutting. Rampant self-sower in Apple-Tree Garden, tiny daisy blooms, nice bouquet filler.
Columbine, see *Aquilegia*				

INDEX TO SOME EXCELLENT PERENNIALS (*Continued*)

NAME BOTANICAL AND COMMON	HEIGHT IN FEET	COLOR	SEASON	REMARKS
Convallaria majalis	1	White	May	Fragrant, open shade, groundcover.
Coralbells, see *Heuchera* *Cowslip*, see *Caltha palustris* Cranesbill, see *Geranium* Daylily, see *Hemerocalis*				
Delphinium grandiflorum (*chinense*)	½–2	Blue, white	June–Oct.	Reliable, intermittent bloom; cut back between bursts. Biennial.
Dianthus	1	Red, pink, white		Many types, lime and grit in soil.
caryophyllus	1		June–Sept.	More humus in soil, fragrant.
plumarius	1–1½		May	Old-fashioned, fragrant, for edging.
Dicentra				
eximia	1–2	Pink	May–Oct.	Plumy type, sun or shade, persistent foliage.
spectabilis	2	Pink	Apr.–June	Handsome but summer disappearance, light shade.
Doronicum, Hybrids	1–1½	Yellow	Apr.–May	Good spring yellow; summer crown only.
Evening Primrose, see *Oenothera* False Dragonhead, see *Physostegia* Feverfew, see *Chrysanthemum parthenium* Forget-me-not, see *Myosotis* Funkia, see *Hosta*				

Gaillardia	2	Red, yellow	June–Nov.	Drought-enduring.
Garden-heliotrope, see *Valeriana*				
Geranium maculatum	1½	Pink-lavender	June	Edging for Fern Path, is cut down after blooming.
Globeflower, see *Trollius*				
Gypsophila 'Bristol Fairy'	2–4	White	June–Oct.	For garden misting and bouquets; cut for repeat bloom.
repens	Creeping	White, pink	June–Sept.	For edging or rock garden.
Helenium autumnale	1–4	Yellow to red	Aug.–Sept.	Showy daisy form; divide every spring.
Helen's-flower, see *Helenium*				
Helianthus decapetalus, 'Flore-pleno'	4	Yellow	July–Sept.	Coarse plant, dahlia flower, rampant but useful.
Heliopsis	3–4	Yellow, orange	July–Nov.	Strong, fine to cut.
Helleborus niger	1–2	Pink-white	Feb.–Mar.	Light shade, evergreen foliage, some years much earlier.
Hemerocallis, Species and Hybrids	1½–4½	Yellow, orange, pink, green tones	May–Oct.	Summer essential, fine foliage and flowers; chart pages 84–85.
Hesperis matronalis	3	White, lavender	June–Sept.	Fragrant.
Heuchera sanguinea	1–1½	Rose, white	June–Aug.	Excellent for edging, enduring foliage.

INDEX TO SOME EXCELLENT PERENNIALS (*Continued*)

NAME BOTANICAL AND COMMON	HEIGHT IN FEET	COLOR	SEASON	REMARKS
Hosta, Species and Hybrids	1–3	White, lavender	July–Aug.	Fine strong foliage, light shade.
Iberis				
'Autumn Snow'	½	White	Apr.–May; Sept.	Three varieties neat and compact, fine for formal edging. 'Purity' a little larger than the others.
'Little Gem'	½	White	May	
'Purity'	½	White	May	
sempervirens	1	White	Apr.–June	Sprawling evergreen species, my favorite edger; requires winter anti-desiccant protection if in sun, not in shade.
Iris				
cristata	3–4 (inches)	Lavender, white	May–June	Shade.
germanica	2–3	Various	May–June	Familiar bearded, chart page 77.
gracilipes	10 (inches)	Pink-lilac	May	Slender iris.
kaempferi	2	Pink, purple, white	June–July	Handsome flat blooms.
reticulata	2	Deep violet	Feb.–Mar.	Netted iris.
sibirica	2–3	Purple, white	June	Grassy foliage.
tectorum	10 (inches)	Lavender, white	Apr.–May	Roof iris of China.
versicolor	2–3	Purple	June–July	Wild blue flag.
Jacob's-Ladder, see *Polemonium reptans*				
Japanese Iris, see *I. kaempferi*				
Larkspur, see *Delphinium*				
Leopardsbane, see *Doronicum*				
Lily-of-the-valley, see *Convallaria majalis*				

Limonium latifolium, see *Statice*	1½	Lavender	July–Aug.	Good for misting, for drying, green crown.
Marsh-marigold, see *Caltha* Meadowrue, see *Thalictrum*				
Mertensia virginica	1½–2	Blue-pink	April	Enchanting for shade, dies down.
Michaelmas daisy, see *Aster*				
Myosotis				
scorpioides (*palustris*)	12–20 (inches)	Blue	Apr.–Sept.	True marsh perennial type.
sylvatica	9–18 (inches)	Blue	June–Aug.	Prefers damp location, semishade, biennial, self-sows.
Oenothera fruticosa	1½	Yellow	June–July	Showy and spreading.
Paeonia				
albiflora (*lactiflora*)	2–3	Red, pink, white	May–June	Familiar Chinese type.
suffruticosa (*moutan*)	3–4	Same, also yellow	May	Tree peony, shrubby.
Papaver orientale	2–3	Red, pink, white	May–June	Dies down after bloom; green winter crown.
Pasqueflower, see *Anemone pulsatilla* Peony, see *Paeonia*				
Phlox				
divaricata	1	Lavender, white	May	Indispensable groundcover for shade.
paniculata	2–4	All but yellow	July–Oct.	Hardy summer phlox, no mildew on 'Star Fire'.
subulata	½	Rose, purple, white	Apr.–May	Creeping mat growth.
suffruticosa	2–4	White	June	Early tall, as 'Miss Lingard'.

INDEX TO SOME EXCELLENT PERENNIALS *(Continued)*

NAME BOTANICAL AND COMMON	HEIGHT IN FEET	COLOR	SEASON	REMARKS
Physostegia virginiana	1½–3	Pink, white	July–Sept.	Coarse, spreading, reliable.
Pinks, see *Dianthus*				
Platycodon grandiflorum	1½	Purple, white	May–Oct.	Fine foliage and flower.
Polemonium reptans	1	Lavender-blue	May–June	Woods or edging plant, dies down then renews.
Poppy, see *Papaver* Primrose, see *Oenothera*				
Primula vulgaris	¾	Yellow	Apr.–May	Woodland, edging for shade.
Sea Lavender, see *Limonium* or *Statice* Shasta Daisy, see *Chrysanthemum maximum* Spiderwort, see *Tradescantia* Spirea, see *Astilbe* *Statice*, see *Limonium latifolium*				
Stokesia	1½	Lavender, white	July–Aug.	Fine in garden, lasting cut flower.
Sunflower, see *Helianthus* or *Heliopsis* Sweet-rocket, see *Hesperis*				
Thalictrum polygamum	8	White	July	Handsome woodland plant.

Thermopsis caroliana	5	Yellow	June–July	Pealike flower.
Tradescantia virginiana, Hybrids	2½	White, pink, purple	May–July; Sept.–Oct.	Shade or sun; cut down, renews late summer; nice for streamside.
Trollius europaeus	2	Yellow, orange	May–July	Fine bloom in light shade with moisture.
Tufted Pansy, see *Viola*				
Valeriana officinalis	4	Blush-white	June–July	Heliotrope scent. Nice in wild garden.
Viola cornuta	½	Yellow, white, purple, apricot	Apr.–Oct.	Charming small perennial pansy, not always heat-resistant.
Windflower, see *Anemone japonica* Yarrow, see *Achillea*				

Skunk-cabbage, the handsome harbinger of spring, opens in April, along the brook bank with clumps of 'White Lady' narcissus nearby. The narrow-leafed dogtooth violets volunteered here and make a yellow-flowered groundcover as the Christmas ferns emerge from winter rest.

7. FERNS ARE FOR EVERYWHERE

Along Paths, in Gardens with Flowers, for Bogs, and Odd Places

Ferns are marvelous plants—beautiful, varied, adaptable, irresistible. Almost untended, they come up every year. In fact, I did not thin out my Fern Garden for seven years. True, it was something of a chore then, dividing some of those handsome mighty growers. It seems to me that ferns belong in every garden. If you are busy and want an effect easily and quickly, ferns are for you; if you are pressed with garden chores and have little outside help, ferns will prove your ally. If you appreciate plants with through-the-season good looks, you can certainly rely on ferns.

In early spring, ferns are delightful as the fiddleheads thrust upward and then unfurl, quite slowly over a matter of weeks, into exquisite and varying types of fronds. In their own haunts, they vary from a few inches to 5 feet (without considering the tropical giants), and the fronds can resemble green lace veiling, as in the maidenhair, or sharply cut, dark green leather, as in the Christmas fern. Some fronds are pale and feathery like those of the lady, New York, or hay-scented; some put up fruiting sprays like "flowers," as the royal and cinnamon ferns. All are fascinating, and in all seasons. When nature seems asleep, the evergreen ferns rise above the first snow. But perhaps they mean most on hot summer days when their green composure is so refreshing. In torrid July, I particularly enjoy the look of the pale green New York fern foaming out under a white birch clump. It just came as a squatter and I let it stay since it does not crowd out the colony of yellow crocuses that I had planted there before.

You can safely set out ferns early in spring or late in fall, though I admit I move them any time that suits my convenience, even late in June. Transplanted in full leaf, they suffer some, but sprayed lightly with the hose every evening for a week or so afterwards, they will survive. Anyway, I have never lost a plant, although I have divided and shifted a multitude of them.

Which Ferns for You?

To select the right ferns, start by deciding what you want them to do for you. The coarse invasive bracken will cover an open sunny meadow or barren bank; the sensitive fern will spread at a great rate in open shade, and you won't want to admit either to your tidy garden. Growing under a fence row, the hay-scented fern will make a lacy ribbon and save you from having to clip grass there. It looks fragile but is strong like a delicate woman who turns out to have a whim of iron. The osmundas—cinnamon, royal, and interrupted—will thrive as they do here with cowslips or marsh-marigolds in a swampy area, being native to rather wet conditions; the polypody will creep over logs and rocks in a rock garden. Although most ferns prefer an acid condition—and revel in it here—there are lovers of limestone, such as the fragile bladder fern that thrives in sweet soil. If you have found shade a problem, almost all ferns will prosper under deciduous trees where many other plants decline.

The growth of ferns is fascinating. In spring the emerging crooks unfurl; in summer, the mature plants dominate; as night grows cool in autumn, they become a golden panorama. And some add fragrance to beauty, as the hay-scented fern whose sweetness is released when we brush by it or press the fronds in a book. The bladder ferns and the New York fern also smell sweet when dried or crushed. And for children, there is the bulblet bladder fern that produces baby ferns from tiny bulbs on the underside of the leaves, and the ebony spleenwort that thrives in a terrarium.

The well-named royal fern, *Osmunda regalis,* revels in the moist, acid soil along the brook, settling beside a tree there in fairly dense shade. Elsewhere, with more light, it reaches 5 feet in colonies of cinnamon and interrupted ferns.

Perhaps you have a piece of woodland on your place and would like to have a garden there predominantly of ferns. If so, choose the shade- and acid-lovers, and arrange them in both related and contrasting foliage groups, perhaps on each side of a wide (at least 4- to 5-foot) grass path. Such a path can be mowed along with the rest of the grass and will serve as transition from lawn to woods.

Where lawn meets woodland, you might plant, as I have, a ground-cover area of Christmas ferns interspersed with clumps of narcissus. Ferns with spring bulbs, wildflowers, or other early perennials make a wonderfully carefree association. As the bulbs retreat and their foliage matures, or as the earliest flowering plants grow shabby, up come those sturdy fern croziers, unfurling at just the most appropriate time. The later emerging shield, bulblet bladder, and New York ferns all make attractive companions for bulbs.

With this fern-and-bulb association, you aren't harassed into cutting down bulb foliage before it has fully ripened since its more unsightly weeks are quite unseen. I grow my Christmas ferns with 'White Lady' narcissus and both plants through the years seem extremely pleased.

Ferns and Azaleas

The planting I call my Fern Garden is not composed entirely of ferns but predominantly so. You pass into this garden via a gently curved grass path, a sentinel white birch clump at the entrance, another at the side of the terminal bed. There the path joins another going to the brook on one side, up three steps to the Round Garden, which also features ferns, on the other.

Beds on each side of the path are a good 9 feet wide to accommodate the somewhat balanced groupings of big osmundas, all great beauties, growing up to 4 feet here in the rich acid soil left when the brook moved back, as I think, to its present narrow channel. On one side the garden slopes *down* to the brook, and there a fine stand of skunk cabbage, that handsome harbinger of spring, opens in early April with plants of false hellebore rising in its midst. On the other side, the garden slopes *up* to a tall stand of the shrubby meadowsweet or sweet pepperbush, *Clethra alnifolia,* which perfumes the July and August air so pleasantly for us in the evening on the porch. Mountain-laurel is planted throughout the Fern Garden to give it winter structure.

Various azaleas thrive in the Fern Garden. Four of the native species grow on the outside of the path near the brook. The pinxterbloom, *Rhododendron nudiflorum,* or wild honeysuckle, opens first, and before it leafs out, usually in early May, a charming 5-foot plant. By mid-May the taller pinkshell azalea, *R. vaseyi,* one of our finest natives, offers light pink blooms, and later rich red autumn foliage.

Early in June two pairs of hybrid azaleas, salmon-pink and white, balanced on each side of the path, make effective accents there. These are followed by the 10-foot extremely fragrant *R. arborescens,* which perfumes the air with showy white flower clusters.

In July the tallest of them all, to 12 feet, the swamp azalea, *R. viscosum,* that revels in this rich moist soil, opens white blooms that are also heavily scented. Throughout July and into August, color is maintained along the path by clumps of daylilies.

But it is in spring that I have now achieved a dramatic effect with an April–May path edging of white and lavender wood-hyacinths,

The lovely variegated fern, *Athyrium goeringianum pictum,* growing beside a flagstone path, fills in an otherwise waste area that was difficult to keep weedfree.

Scilla campanulata, and the pink-lavender wild geranium. For almost a month these are enchanting companions and they have taught me a lesson; plant a lot of a few things for grand effect, instead of spotting many different plants just because they are so appealing to you. Behind this colorful edging are massed Christmas, royal, and cinnamon ferns. They take over effectively when the fading scillas and geraniums are cut back. A few volunteering purple *Iris versicolor* provide a good foliage contrast of lance leaves to fern fronds.

In any woods garden volunteers like this iris appear; most of them have been welcome here but not that heartless invader, goutweed. Two appreciated newcomers are the dogtooth violets, a sheet of yellow in April, and the tall, ferny, summer-flowering meadowrue, *Thalictrum polygamum,* with creamy sprays of terminal bloom. This meadowrue, growing to 8 feet, requires staking as it towers above ferns and daylilies.

The terminal bed of the Fern Garden is a mass of royal ferns luxuriating in the dampness and yellow evening primroses, an effective June picture clearly visible from the house, which is some 40 feet away. Because of its carrying quality, yellow is a good choice for

Ferns were often used as foundation plants beside old New England houses. Here the strong cinnamon fern rises in the corner, with the lovely lacy maidenhair at the edge, and Solomon's-seal and Jack-in-the-pulpit plants in between.

any flowers you want to see from a distance. On that account I have planted yellow daylilies for July and August to scatter color among the ferns.

Of course, white can also be seen at the end of the path, and the white Japanese iris in the terminal bed is quite effective. Wet in spring, well drained in summer, with adequate sun and very rich, acid soil, this is a lovely place for Japanese iris, and also for the earlier white astilbe which itself has such ferny foliage. You will enjoy both as companions for your ferns.

The Round Garden

I spoke of the three steps at the left of the fern path. These lead to a little hidden Round Garden. You'd never know it was there unless you wandered up the steps or followed the outside flagstone path that seems to lead nowhere. However, behind the concealing mountain-laurel, holly, and spreading dogwood is this really secret garden, just 24 feet across. The beds are filled with wood-hyacinths (from divisions of the fern-path planting) and Christmas ferns, a satisfactory association, the second concealing the demise of the first, with lavender Jacob's-ladder making a pretty edging and colonies of trillium, galax, and bloodroot at the entrance.

Laurel defines the outer circle, with blue and white hostas following the inside curve. It is very shady in this little plot. In June a white fringetree on one side of a plank seat drenches it with fragrance. A yellow vernal witch-hazel on the other side (visible early in March from the house) invites cold weather investigation and rewards with a sweet yeasty aroma. A giant Norway maple, pruned to a sculptured form, rises in perspective at the back.

The seat is nothing more than a 1- by 6-foot plank set on 2-foot lengths of standard sewer pipe sunk about halfway in the ground. Despite its low origins, the bench looks nice and so relaxing that even I have found time to sit on it. If you have room, I am sure you too would enjoy one small secluded garden particularly your own for escape and thought.

Ferns for Accent and Mingling

The larger ferns also make fine specimens in the manner of small shrubs. Because these big growers will tolerate so much shade, they

The Round Garden is so enclosed and secluded you would not find it unless you happened to wander into it along the flagstone path. From the plank seat, shaded on the right by a fringe-tree, birds and birdbath at the side, you can see the plant room in full sun. Bradbury photo.

are also fine for odd places where you don't want to go groping in after weeds. I planted an interrupted fern in a corner behind the wisteria, a cinnamon fern against the house in back of a viburnum bush, and both of these in a very shady spot under a maple as backdrop for a forward, sun-reaching planting of daylilies.

Ferns can also be mingled with evergreens in foundation plantings. In New England, they used to be planted alone along the front of white colonial houses with ancient lilacs at the corners. Here I have seen the hay-scented fern planted to retain a bank and combined with cinnamon and interrupted ferns and pink climbing roses along a tottering wall. Bright-colored coleus or impatiens with ferns make charming plantings, especially in shade, and at the seashore, the interrupted fern endures the sun.

The "common" maidenhair, is surely the most beguiling of ferns, its wiry stems and flat whirls of fronds unique. After seeing it in Vermont in the wild, a great bank of it above a stream, I began to fit it in here wherever there was space, under trees, among rhododendron and laurel, at the edge of the bog garden, close to places I frequent. I can never have enough of the maidenhair but it spreads slowly, first making only a handsome single plant. In any case, if I had to select one fern as my favorite, it would be this elegant plant.

For rock gardens, there are many treasures that naturally seek the companionship of rocks and boulders. Ebony spleenwort, polypody, bladder ferns, and shield ferns are all possibilities to plant with your forget-me-nots, small phloxes, Jacob's-ladder, primroses, violets, and veronicas. Of course, the larger maidenhair, but hardly to 24 inches, belongs here, too. Plant it in descending order and it will look like a cool green waterfall coming over the rocks. I have already mentioned the value of ferns as groundcovers, the invasive types—bracken, sensitive, ostrich, and hay-scented—for broad areas. For controlled coverage, I'd choose the Christmas fern.

The only thing I have against ferns is their jaw-breaking names; on that account, the chart below is by common name. I have a friend who in moments of extreme frustration uses *Polystichum acrostichoides* as a swear word. Shouted with feeling, it is most expressive.

Aside from the nomenclature, which the botanists make worse by changing it all the time, ferns are perfect. However, like all that lives, they need *some* care. When the new fronds are well developed, I cut off the old basal fronds if the plants are prominently placed among perennials or bordering a shrub bed. Along the Fern Walk, I let the old fronds stay and I mulch heavily with pine needles after my spring attack on the goutweed. (The mulch mitigates the menace; it does not eradicate it.) Decayed leaves are another good mulch for ferns, but don't let a heavy mat of fresh oak leaves accumulate, for while rotting they will damp out the less vigorous species of ferns. In times of drought, I see to it that my ferns get a good deep soaking about once a week. This is essential. In general, they prefer a humusy soil with plenty of leafmold, and they don't mind a mixing in of some stones, which is lucky for me at Stony Brook. No fertilizer is ever needed.

SOME BEAUTIFUL AND USEFUL FERNS

This chart is by common name because most of the botanical names are so difficult and unfamiliar.
*E—Evergreen; D—Deciduous

NAME	HEIGHT IN INCHES	FOLIAGE TYPE*	LIGHT REQUIREMENT	SOIL	BEHAVIOR AND APPEARANCE	REMARKS
Bladder Fern, Bulblet *Cystopteris bulbifera*	18–30	D	Shade.	Neutral or sweet; not acid; best on weathered limestone.	Long narrow tapering fronds; pinkish stems; yellow-green fronds; produces baby ferns from bulblets; amusing to children.	For rock garden or to shade soil for clematis or other lime-lovers; naturalizes readily, appears 4 to 6 weeks after fragile bladder fern.
Bladder Fern, Fragile *Cystopteris fragilis*	4–12	D	Shade, sensitive to drought; may discolor.	Rocks, ledges, sometimes moist stony woods.	Deeply toothed, green; spreads into crevices.	Early croziers uncurl before other ferns, late March, good cover for earliest bulbs.
Bracken or Brake Fern *Pteridium aquilinum*	36–48	D	Part shade or full sun, open hillsides, pastures, banks.	Anywhere, acid or alkaline, even in sterile areas.	Triangular fronds, creeper, violent, coarse grower.	Too invasive for home garden, has uses elsewhere.
Christmas Fern *Polystichum acrostichoides*	15–30	E	Open shade here under dogwoods and witch-hazel, beneath cliff.	Fairly damp, rich leafmold, but adaptable.	Refined, crown spreads slowly; fine ground cover. Evergreen until midwinter.	Edge of my woodland, interplanted with narcissus.
Cinnamon Fern *Osmunda cinnamomea*	24–60	D	Open.	Requires rich acid soil and moisture, native	Mighty native grower where conditions suit;	Fine bold accent; showiest fiddleheads; "cinnamon

				to bogs.	crown, looks tropical.	stick" sterile fronds; lovely with daylilies.
Ebony Spleenwort *Asplenium platyneuron*	8–20	E	Light shade.	Stony or sandy leafmold; acid or alkaline.	Narrow, dark green fronds in a crown.	Pretty for a rock garden; nice in terrariums.
Goldie Fern *Dryopteris goldiana*	24–48	D	Shade.	Rich humus, neutral to slightly acid, requires moisture.	Dark yellow-green broad oval fronds, lighter beneath.	Palmlike and tropical, fine specimen type; considered by some our most beautiful native fern.
Hay-scented Fern *Dennstaedtia punctilobula*	12–36	D	Shade or sun; good soil-holder for exposed slopes.	Good on poor soil; wild invasive grower in acid, more circumspect in sweet.	Feathery, yellow-green, creeping, spreads from root mats; rampant.	Aroma of hay in sun or when drying; in fall, turns light rust color.
Interrupted Fern *Osmunda claytoniana*	30–36	D	Shade or sun.	Deep rich soil, acid, moist, native in swampy places.	Somewhat coarse fronds, good specimen plant, crown, yellow-green to dark.	Fertile frond "interrupted" by separate branchlets of spore cases; interesting growth.
Japanese Painted Fern *Athyrium goeringianum*	18–24	D	Open shade.	Leafmold on acid side, adaptable if moist.	Spreads slowly, makes a clump not a whorl.	Gray-green with silver markings; fine accent plant, as beside a rock.
Lady Fern *Athyrium filix-femina*	12–36	D	Partial shade or full sun.	Dry to wet woods.	Yellow-green to medium, older leaves brownish, finely cut, creeping.	Adaptable, sometimes too strong in volunteering; hardly ladylike, more Women's Lib.

SOME BEAUTIFUL AND USEFUL FERNS (*Continued*)

NAME	HEIGHT IN INCHES	FOLIAGE TYPE*	LIGHT REQUIRE-MENT	SOIL	BEHAVIOR AND APPEARANCE	REMARKS
Maidenhair Fern *Adiantum pedatum*	8–20	D	Woods, dense shade.	Moist, neutral, rich leafmold, drainage important.	Creeping, unique, dainty circular lacy tops; wiry dark stems.	Early appearance, light to medium green, lovely with spring wildflowers or shrubs.
New York Fern *Dryopteris noveboracensis*	8–24	E	Open shade.	Adaptable, late in coming up, about mid-May, turns brown early.	Shallow creeper, delicate light green, harmless among stronger plants.	Excellent ground-cover; fronds taper both ends; lovely contrast to deeper greens.
Ostrich Fern *Matteuccia pensylvanica*	24–48	D	Shade to full sun if near water.	Deep, rich soil, moist to wet for streamsides.	Plumy vase form but creeps by ropelike stolons, even under paving; turns brown early.	Not for refined locations; hard to eliminate but attractive where plenty of room; looks like an ostrich plume.
Polypody *Polypodium virginianum*	3–10	E	Light shade.	On rocks in moderately dry leafmold; sometimes on fallen logs.	Dense spreading mats, a creeper; yellow to medium green.	Darling small fern for right environment.
Royal Fern *Osmunda regalis*	24–48	D	Light to dense shade.	Moist, acid soil; in drier locations only with special care.	Brown spore clusters like flowers; vase form, fine for	Graceful for a bank planting or along a path; mixes well with cinnamon

					contrast. Native in swampy places; young fronds wine-red.	and interrupted, or with Japanese iris and astilbe.
Sensitive Fern *Onoclea sensibilis*	12–36	D	Shade or in full sun.	Bog or drier soil; best as bank-holder along water.	Rampant creeper; coarse, showy, not for small garden.	Yellow-green, "sensitive" to drought and first frost—good texture contrast, browns early; fertile fronds good for flower arrangements.
Shield Fern, Intermediate (Evergreen Wood Fern) *Dryopteris intermedia*	16–32	E	Partial shade.	Moist, rich in humus.	Deeply cut, dark green, prickly fronds.	Late to emerge so excellent planted with early bulbs.
Shield Fern, Marginal (Leather Wood Fern) *Dryopteris marginalis*	12–36	E	Shade but adaptable.	Rich wood soil, rocky shelters.	Blue-green, fronds in vase form, very lovely, crown.	Firm texture, not toothed; fruit dots underneath along margins of leaflet.
Shield Fern, Spinulose (Toothed Wood Fern) *Dryopteris spinulosa*	14–28	Evergreen sterile fronds; deciduous fertile ones.	Among rocks and trees.	Acid, moist, but adaptable.	Circular clumps, lighter green than *D. intermedia*, very lovely, crown.	Volunteered under my apple tree and along wall; also on edge of bog garden; lacy but less so than *D. intermedia*.
Wood Ferns (see Shield Ferns)						

From the kitchen casements there is a view of the always-in-bloom Look-Into Garden. Here in summer under the shade of the white birch, impatiens plants—white, pink, and lavender—bloom in carefree abundance.

8. *MY SMALL LOOK-INTO AND APPLE-TREE GARDENS*

February-to-Frost Color Sequences

Despite the need to keep our plantings in workable bounds, most of us want one or two colorful masses of flowers, these to take the place of the long perennial borders or formal gardens we may once have managed. Although I dignify my Look-Into and Apple-Tree plots as "gardens," this really is pretentious, for they are nothing more than informal plantings with the emphasis on flowers.

If you have a boundary planting of small trees and shrubs, you may want to extend it with bulbs and a few perennials and annuals as I have the Look-Into Garden along my driveway; if you have a *deep-rooted* shade tree, with enough light coming through the branches naturally (or let through by pruning), you might enjoy an arrangement like my Apple-Tree Garden for shade plants.

My Look-Into Garden

What is important when you reduce flower beds to reduce work is to have the flowers you do have in full view. With this in mind I developed my Look-Into Garden, widening the narrow tree-and-shrub driveway bed, incorporating some of the shaded grass area on the open side, and introducing a quantity of flowers for color. This is the only place I bother with succession of bloom—spring bulbs followed by summer annuals with chrysanthemums for the autumn weeks. I work in this garden with more satisfaction than elsewhere since it is small enough for me, singlehanded, to keep it in the pink. And that it must be, for I look into it at every meal, in fact, with every cup of coffee. A weed there is a personal affront.

The clump of white birch at the near end is handsome in every season and in all weather I dwell on it with pleasure. Then for eight to nine months of the year—the length of time depends somewhat on weather—I enjoy a panorama of bloom. A landscape architect friend scorns my "bits-and-pieces approach," as she calls this miscellany of mine with its floral purpose. She urges me to plant my border in solid greens, for the "sake of the overall design." But in such a small space you cannot have much design if you also want some of this and that for seasonal color. To my mind, if a planting is somehow balanced, as this is, by a similar *form* of bed on the opposite side of the lawn and with at least one element repeated, as a crab apple at the end of each area, then sufficient attention has been paid to design.

From Winter to Spring

It's the cold-weather flowers that are a special joy. In February the winter aconites open bright golden blooms among the Christmas ferns that serve as carpeting wherever there is room in this necessarily crowded arrangement. This *Eranthis hyemalis* is too little known but always admired by visitors when the cheerful buttercups peer out of their lacy green collars. These are "permanent" bulbs, selfsowing and spreading so that an original dozen soon becomes an appreciated fifty.

Plant the tiny tubers (they aren't true bulbs) as early in fall as you can get them, about 3 inches deep and a little farther apart. Perhaps you can include some of the other winter gems I have planted elsewhere but all close to the house—'Yellow Mammoth' crocus and the lavender *C. tomasinianus,* snowdrops, *Galanthus nivalis,* and that choice, very early, little fragrant *Iris unguicularis* (*I. stylosa*), which in some years surprises me as early as January. But with this one, you take a chance. Even planted in sun, and close to a warm house wall it does not always survive.

Along with my aconites come the so-called Christmas roses. I've seen pictures of these blooming in snow but doubt if it is December snow. Even my well-established plants, at least ten years in the same on-view spot, usually do not open their lovely waxen cups before February. And how those flowers endure bad weather, holding their own and turning deeper and deeper pink.

Do plant this *Helleborus niger* where you can see it from the house. My plants flourish in the open shade of the two flowering trees in the driveway bed and I take care to water them *deeply* in summer when they are producing more of their handsome and truly evergreen palmate leaves.

Next in March comes the Cornelian-cherry, a flowering tree I hold by pruning to 15 feet and cherish for its cloud of tiny, pale yellow petalless flowers, to be followed by red fruits in summer.

Soon the ribbon-petaled, marvelously fragrant star magnolia dares the frost, or at least it used to. After twelve lovely years my plant succumbed to an extremely cold winter, but I will plant it again. In wet seasons, the flowers of *Magnolia stellata* may turn brown but in at least two out of three years mine always made it, glistening with white bloom for about two March-into-April weeks. Then the leaves pushed out and the flowers faded.

Spring

April is full of pictures with early emphasis on the stalwart Dutch hyacinths whose fragrance is so "free on the air," a delight to all who pass, and also to me when it's warm enough to open the casements and let the hyacinth scent drift into the kitchen. The blue 'Côte d'Azur' opens just under the windows, pinks and blues on the north side of the driveway bed, colonies of whites and blues on the inside of the bed, and at the end an arresting Turkish-carpet motif of white 'L'Innocence' hyacinths, bright blue *Scilla sibirica,* and the early red *Tulipa praestans.*

The other flowering tree of my planting is the silverbell or snowdrop-tree, *Halesia carolina.* Do discover it if you haven't already. It is choice. Hung with white bells from late April well into May, it is a lovely sight. I prune it to 20 feet, keeping growth high and open, as with *Cornus mas,* so that light and air come through to plants of the fragrant, old-fashioned lemon-lily *Hemerocallis flava,* one of the rare yellows of this season.

Spring into Summer

May is not a month of sequences but a grand all-at-once burgeoning that slides into the luxury of June. Now the mountain-laurel, *Kalmia latifolia,* opens pink-tinted, white shells of bloom. I prune the plants right after bloom to control their spread and height as well. The laurel along with two plants of evergreen Japanese holly, *Ilex crenata microphylla,* gives ballast to the planting and cuts off the view of the drive from my kitchen rocker.

The hardy candytuft, *Iberis sempervirens,* makes the border, and I like the sprawly species rather than the neat cultivars. This candytuft, a white foam of May bloom, binds the bed all round, delineating it from lawn. It is my favorite edger but it does require the winter protection of an anti-desiccant; otherwise plants in the sun, not those in the shade, may turn brown. Cut back, they readily renew but then the flowers are lost for that spring. Covered with Wilt-Pruf, Formula NCF, early in December and again on a 45-degree day in February, they come through winter unharmed.

The tall May tulips bloom with the candytuft. The bulbs, planted 10 to 12 inches deep, do not "run out." Mine after five years are going strong. Where I can, I set them in circles with space in the center for a well-started petunia or impatiens that goes in long before I dare remove the maturing bulb foliage. I put more petunias at the edge of the bed where they get some sun. Impatiens needs no sun and is a boon to all who must garden in shade. You can buy in-flower plants from a nursery or roadside stand when it's safe to set out plants. Or you can sow seeds of these slow annuals indoors about eight weeks ahead of settled weather in your area; more than eight weeks means too much indoor transplanting or else weak leggy plants.

I like to select matching colors for the two annuals and to repeat bocks of six plants of each color. One year it was 'Elfin Salmon' impatiens with 'Maytime' petunias—'Coral Magic' petunias would be as good a match. Another time 'Elfin Pink' impatiens with 'Chiffon Cascade' petunias for a paler effect. For a white I like 'Park's Snowflake'. Combinations of purples and pinks also appeal to me.

Since you may have only one planting of annuals, try to limit the number of colors so as to get a strong effect. I could not resist a few accent plants of blue lobelia, also shade-tolerant, and at the sunny end of this garden I put in three tall yellow marguerites (*Chrysanthemum frutescens*). The impatiens conveniently discards faded flowers, also seeds itself madly. To keep petunias in health and looks, likewise the marguerites, snip off faded blooms and regularly trim plants back a little. Give all annuals a dose of liquid fertilizer every three to four weeks. This will insure fine bloom right up to frost.

Two lilacs, the single purple 'Ludwig Spaeth', and the single white 'Vestale' open in May-to-June weeks. Once in five years or so I cut some of the heaviest growth to the ground to control their exuberance. The lilacs bloom along with the Japanese crab apple at the terminous of the bed, and in every season this slow-growing, roundheaded *Malus floribunda* is a joy—heavy with pink bloom early in May, bright with red fruits from late August into October, nice foliage all season.

In summer the ancient apple tree, pruned to open shade, shelters a cool colony of ferns, pale yellow daylilies, white flowering tobacco, and a few late golden doronicums. Gottscho-Schleisner photo.

Peonies are lined along the driveway site, and a few set on the south side, too, opening usually around Memorial Day and continuing into June. The double, red-flecked white 'Festiva Maxima', the pink 'Mons. Jules Élie' and 'Thérèse', and the single, deep pink 'Sea Shell' with its prominent golden stamens look lovely there. I do not see 'Thérèse' on growers' lists these days but it is a lucious pink peony of the same shade as *Dianthus plumarius* 'Beatrix'. This sprawls over the curbing below 'Thérèse' and holds steady green growth through winter. (For the elusive 'Beatrix' you can substitute, if you must, 'Salmon Unique'.)

Summer to Frost

In July the pink daylily 'Evelyn Claar' blooms on the driveway side and, opposite, under the silverbell-tree, a great clump of the 18-inch purple balloon-flower, *Platycodon*. This is a good accent plant that continues into August if seedpods are not allowed to form.

The last shrub to bloom is the *Franklinia* (*Gordonia*) *alatamaha* with white, kid-glove cups that open in succession from early August until frost. I don't let it get much above 5 feet and cherish it for its late flowering habit, its rarity, and the fine, sweet, tea fragrance.

Somehow I find room for a number of chrysanthemum plants I buy late in September in tones of russet and gold. These are selected with quantities of buds that will open through October and sometimes up to Thanksgiving. I set the pots on top of the ground, where I must remember to water them, for there isn't room for direct planting into the bed. Chrysanthemums offer the last color for my so-satisfactory eight-to-nine months Look-Into Garden. The stage is then left to the evergreen foliage of ilex, mountain-laurel, and candytuft, and to the white, four-trunked birch until the next spring—less than four months away.

This kind of planting takes thought, so work yours out on paper first, as I did, and don't mind discarding and substituting plants if dull weeks occur. I've been operating on my Look-Into Garden for more than a decade. I hope I can leave it alone now for a few years.

Apple-Tree Garden

Perhaps you have a fine, deep-rooted shade tree on your place that can be the setting for your colorful mass of flowers. Although one

For autumn color in the Apple-Tree Garden, pots of russet, gold, and white chrysanthemums are set on top of the bed which is so thickly set with other plants that there is no space to insert them. The chrysanthemums, kept well watered, last for a month—one of my minor horticultural extravagances—and the coralbells make a neat almost evergreen edging.

swallow does not make a summer nor one crow a winter, you will find that one tree can make a garden. My apple tree does this almost by itself, as I see its beauty changing through the seasons from stark and handsome silhouette to new leaves, a veil of blossoms, and finally globes of green fruit like ornaments on a Christmas tree. As a canopy for a small garden, an apple tree is charming. An old specimen has always been part of my planning. I think of the first garden that was really mine—"Orchard Edge" the place was called—for along the side was an ancient orchard planted to sod. A cool and pleasant outdoor living room it was and, as garden background, a lovely sight.

Then in my second garden, miraculously I was again possessed of a single ancient tree, gnarled and dignified, long past its youthful prime. The tree man patched it up and chained the weakest limb. Then one summer night in a thunderstorm, as I stood alone on the wide verandah, watching the fury of the elements playing about my treasured tree, there was suddenly a great flash of fire, a mighty rending, and before my eyes a great limb—the very arch of my garden—split apart and fell with a terrifying crash. It was as if God spoke there in the empty garden and with His hand parted the bough. I stood transfixed with awe and wonder. Next day we cut the limb cleanly off and sawed it into logs for burning on winter nights. To my mind, there is nothing like apple wood for fires, but I sighed for my lost garden beauty.

My present Apple-Tree Garden is the most satisfactory of all, and it should be, for I have long been experimenting to make it carefree. In fact, the present 8-by-21-foot area of flowers is what remains of an extensive perennial border that terminated here.

An apple tree has the necessary deep roots that do not compete with plantings beneath. It has also high and fairly open shade, and I prune to keep it so. Furthermore, I let the bed stretch out a little at one end into the sun so that I have deep shade, partial shade, and sunshine. Thus various favorite plants can be accommodated.

The May picture under the apple-blossom veil includes white and pink tulips and the incomparable, yellow-shaded 'Gudoshnik' tulip, colonies of tall pink bleedinghearts and Virginia bluebells, all carpeted by selfsowing, true-blue forget-me-nots. I can't forgo the spring harmony these make although the mertensia is cut down after two or three weeks and the bleedinghearts by the end of June. Meanwhile the forget-me-nots are going to seed, and producing a pretty ratty effect but it doesn't last too long, and finally the seeds are cast. Seedlings now spring up in the bed, and also outside, with a crop in all sizes by September. Weeding among them is tedious, only ameliorated by firm fixation on how lovely the forget-me-nots looked in spring.

By July in the front of the bed the blue wave of forget-me-nots is followed by white billows of feverfew, *Chrysanthemum parthenium,* with its tight little white bouquets. This also selfsows. Along the edge the pink clouds of coralbells open on plants that are always in good condition. These two, feverfew and coralbells, to a degree conceal the devastation of seedheads and yellow bulb foliage in back. Meanwhile the big yellow daylilies are opening, and the background ferns, Interrupted and Goldies, have taken a firm stand as green support until frost. The autumn view is strengthened here, as in the Look-Into Garden, just across the driveway, by pots of chrysanthemums in the same rich hues.

If you plan a garden under an apple or other deep-rooted tree, as an ash or sweetgum, prepare the soil well beforehand, loosening it as far down as you can and working in plenty of compost. This is really your only chance to condition the soil. If it is well fertilized each spring and as much mulch spread as seedlings permit, you can develop a colorful display without too much effort. In this garden I used to include gasplant, beebalm, trollius, Jacob's-ladder, and other shade-tolerant perennials, along with the annual flowering tobacco, but I have allowed them to be crowded out in the interest of a stronger effect with fewer kinds and less work.

I should say this about gardening under an apple tree: the steady gathering of the fruit crop through summer offers considerable bending exercise. I tried having the tree sprayed with a fruit retardant but the timing for this is so exacting, it was never successful. As it is, I do have the tree sprayed twice to keep it pestfree, but two sprayings do not, of course, produce edible fruit. That takes twelve, I understand. Anyway the purpose of my Apple-Tree Garden is not a harvest but a mass color at the kitchen door, and that is vividly supplied.

A stone-edged bed of Hybrid Tea roses, with a border of violas and a background of clematis, is close to the house for pleasure and easy care and takes the place of a once extensive formal rose garden with a particularly felicitous association of vine and rose plants. The white birch clump at the side shades the terrace but not the roses.

9. *ROSES—A NEW APPROACH FOR A PLANTED PLACE*

Selection and Care on the Pleasure Principle

Roses are plants that stimulate horticultural passion. Like the man who claimed beef was meat, all else substitute, the ardent rosarian cares only for roses; other plants there may be but not for him. And no effort is too great in the year-round program aimed at the blue ribbon or the silver bowl. First comes the well-prepared bed, dug 2½ to 3 feet deep, then the careful pruning, then pest-and-disease controls with a special preparation for each ailment, and devices for winter protection you'd hardly believe. When I read what the experts do with roses, it makes me ache all over.

For me roses, like other plants, are grown on the pleasure principle. In my day I've had two charming, little formal, box-enclosed rose gardens. Each had four oblong beds for Hybrid Teas, a round center bed of Polyanthas with a birdbath, a Rose Tree in each corner, and grass for carpeting. If roses are your favorite flower and you can give the time to an all-rose garden, a layout like this will give you great pleasure.

In the Landscape

Today on the planted place a more comfortable plan is to use roses less formally. For instance, you can fit them nicely into your foundation area, reserving a section just for roses. A friend has an attractive planting, mainly of Hybrid Teas, filling a triangular space along the walk to her front door. Large-flowered pink, blue, and white clematis trained against the house wall make a beautiful mid-June picture with the roses, which continue to be colorful until frost.

Perhaps you would like to line a curving path, with low Floribundas like 'Coral Glo', 'Goldilocks', or 'Rosenelfe', or a driveway with one of the medium-tall pink blends like 'Fashion' or 'Betty Prior', or plant a hedge of the tall, medium-pink, very lovely 'Little Darling'. To satisfy your urge for a "garden" of roses, how about a bed at the edge of your terrace or below it where you could enjoy the flowers at close view? Less than a dozen well-grown plants would give a fine effect and, if the bed is sheltered by the terrace wall, you could enjoy roses even into November. A reliable, not-too-new, inexpensive selection might include the tall, warm-pink-blend 'Queen Elizabeth' and the orange-blend 'Tropicana' for the back; for the center, the highly fragrant red 'Chrysler Imperial', pink-blend 'First Prize', yellow-to-cream-pink 'Peace', and salmon-pink 'Chicago Peace'; 'Pascali', if you want a white; then one variety of some low clustered flowered rose along the edge for unity. The up-to-2-foot, cream-pink-gold sweetheart rose, 'Cécile Brunner', the orange-red 'Gloria Mundi', or my old favorite, the utterly reliable, though somewhat taller, light pink 'Grüss an Aachen', would look nice. What you select for this limited little rose garden depends on your own color preference. I always get lost in the yellows like 'Golden Masterpiece' myself, but the yellows and whites are the least dependable of roses.

Of course, you will want a climber or two. Before I knocked out the front of my house to build the plant room, I trained and nailed a fragrant "Golden Climber" ("Mrs. Arthur Curtiss James") against the house around the south guest-room window, and it was a joy there. I also favor the rampant blush-pink repeater 'New Dawn', 'Thor', with red blooms that do not fade and appear for six handsome weeks from late May on, and the white 'City of York'. Allow 12 to 15 feet for each of these. The Climbing Hybrid Teas are moderate growers and can be set 6 feet apart. 'Parade' grows to 8 feet,

Four favorite old roses grow in full sun. *Above: left,* the scented, soft pink Hybrid Musk 'Penelope', 5 to 8 feet; *right,* the heavily scented pink Crested Moss, 4 to 5 feet. *Below: left,* the very-fragrant Hybrid Tea, 'Reichspräsident von Hindenburg', 3 to 5 feet with peony-size blooms; *right,* the perfumed lilac pink Rugosa 'Will Alderman', 3 to 5 feet, and it blooms all summer. Courtesy Will Tillotson's Roses.

offers spicy, deep pink flowers in heavy spring-and-fall bursts with some bloom in between, and it thrives even in semishade. 'Climbing Mrs. Sam McGredy' is a lovely orange blend, nice with 'Climbing Summer Snow'.

But if you want only one rose, do choose 'The Fairy', an invincible pink-clustered Polyantha that seems never to be out of bloom, June to November. It is well suited to planting as a specimen beside a door or in a row below the big glass windows of a contemporary house, as it is next door. I view it there with increasing admiration. It thrives in sun or light shade, in good soil or mediocre, and can be pruned to any size you wish.

As Shrubs

If you think of roses as the shrubs they really are and not plants for special, by-themselves plantings, you will realize at once the value of the big 5-to-7-foot growers. Spring bloomers like the fragrant yellow 'Frühlingsmorgen' surpass any forsythia that ever graced a neighbor's yard, 'Sparrieshoop', shrub or climber, with clusters of fragrant soft pink, wavy-petaled, almost single flowers all summer, and the elegant white, red-splashed single flowers of 'Nevada' make a garden by themselves. The tall Hybrid Musks, pink 'Belinda' and salmon-to-white 'Penelope', are so gorgeous no one ever believes them true. "Are those big beautiful bushes *roses*?" the astounded visitor asks.

An eyesore may offer opportunity for roses—the uncompromising lines of a garage yield to the trellised climbing rose; the rough, unsightly bank never properly graded is ideal for the trailing, white Memorial Rose, *Rosa wichuraiana*. On my back hill the broad flights of steps that interrupt the transverse paths rise between banks of this and 'Max Graf'. A thorny hedge of tall Floribundas affords privacy along the good-fence, good-neighbor line. And a compost pile may

If you want only one rose, do select this Polyantha 'The Fairy', invincible and pink clustered; it is never out of bloom, June to November, and it requires minimum attention. Courtesy Will Tillotson's Roses.

require an intercession planting of 'Sarah Van Fleet', or something else tall and lovely.

In the entrance to the meadow, I have two shrub roses that have had the barest minimum of care, and no spraying. The 8-foot Rugosa rose bears some flowers all the time, nice semidouble, fragrant, deep pink ones. Beside it the low 'Frau Dagmar Hartopp' is a very fragrant, five-petaled clear pink with big, glowing, rose hips in fall, and 'Blanc Double de Coubert' so fragrant two of the white blooms

Reaching over the fence toward the sun, this light pink Hybrid Tea Climber charms those who live within and those who pass without.

'Sparrieshoop', shrub or climber, produces clusters of fragrant bright-to-soft pink, almost single flowers all summer on 3- to 4-foot canes—a bouquet rose of charm and elegance. Courtesy Will Tillotson's Roses.

perfume the whole kitchen if I keep the doors closed. Elsewhere the tall, single, yellow *Rosa hugonis* with fine, feathery foliage blooms only in spring, a glorious sight; nearby for June is the fragrant, pink, double 'Crested Moss', and 'Reichspräsident von Hindenburg' (which needs a simpler name if it's ever to be popular). I love it for its reaching damask fragrance and enormous pink blooms with a darker reverse. It grows to about 4 feet here. These shrub roses, old and new, can be extremely tempting, and a catalogue like *Roses of Yesterday and Today* from Tillotson's can set you dreaming—and ordering.

For Accents and Arrangers

Roses can be combined with annuals or used as accents in deep perennial plantings. Tubs of roses are charming on a sunny terrace. Pools in gardens suggest the charm of reflected roses—a double pleasure, so to speak. An irregular pool in the corner of a small plot is all the prettier for a clump of the spicy-scented, velvety crimson 'World's Fair'.

Then we all want roses for cutting to make simple bouquets for the home or important arrangements for flower shows. I do enjoy one rose in a choice little Baccarat bud vase or a bowl of them with

Beside a broad flight of steps, a planting of roses—the handsome pink Grandiflora 'Camelot' and the brilliant red Hybrid Tea 'Christian Dior' —make an arresting garden accent. At the top of the wall two Floribundas—the pink 'Fashion' and brilliant red 'Europeana'—make a fine hedge. Courtesy Star Roses.

Protected from the wind by a high fence, roses flourish in raised beds, edged with wooden strips, and alone make an interesting garden with a pebble center untroubled by mowing or clipping. Courtesy American Association of Nurserymen.

garden flowers on the dining table. The possibilities are infinite, but what isn't is our time and space. If roses are to be a pleasure, we must not always be working with them, but often just looking at them.

The Basics

Most roses need sun for at least half the day, a free circulation of air to avoid mildew and black spot that thrive in damp close quarters, freedom from competing tree roots, and good soil. Prepare the bed, raised 8 to 12 inches if drainage is in question, about two spade lengths deep with a liberal amount of compost or peatmoss worked in. Roots establish quickly in such a mixture. Let the soil settle a week or so before planting. Then early in spring—or fall for second choice—set out your plants, having soaked the roots first in a pail of water. While you work, take care to keep plants covered; exposure to sun or wind is damaging to roots.

Here we place each plant in a hole with the graft or "bud," the knob you see on the stem, just at ground level or barely covered with soil. (In colder climates the graft must be covered with 2, even 3 inches of soil.) Make a cone of soil in each hole to support the roots so that they can spread away from the stem, out and down at a 45-degree angle. Sift soil in around them. Make sure there are no air pockets left in the hole. Work soil in among the roots with your fingers, firming well as you go. When you have filled the hole half-way with soil and all roots are covered, tread the soil down firmly. If you can lift out the plant with one hand, it isn't set firmly enough, so keep going.

Next, fill the hole half full of water. Then go on to the next hole and the next plant, and so on. After the water drains away, go back and fill up each hole with soil—loosely. When you have finished the batch, draw soil up around the stems, heaping it as high as possible, but at least to 4 inches to keep tops from drying out before new roots are able to supply them with moisture. Leave a saucer around the hilled soil for watering till the plant is established. Once the exposed section of the new bushes shows signs of growth, push back the soil you drew up around the canes.

To *prevent* pest and disease, you may have to spray or dust every week or so with an all-purpose preparation; do follow the directions. Even fifty plants take less than half an hour once you get set with a good sprayer or duster and know how to handle your material. And you may be able to avoid much of this with the new fertilizer-systemic preparations that feed plants and control pests at the same time. Worked into the soil around the bushes, and watered in well, these preparations have a long residual affect, for the insecticides are drawn up into the tissues of the plants and stay there. Friends who have tried this, report that two doses—one in early spring and one in July —protected their plants throughout the growing season. Systemic fungicides like Benlate for control of blackspot and mildew are also becoming available, but it is recommended that these be sprayed on the plants not worked into the soil. However, some trials are in process for watering the soil around plants with a Benlate solution, an easier procedure than spraying.

As for pruning, Hybrid Teas, Floribundas, and Polyanthas can be treated about the same—with three-to-four-caned open centers. In spring the canes on Hybrid Teas are shortened to sound wood, cuts being made just above a leaf node. Polyanthas, because of their twiggy tendency, require more thinning out than the others. Let the Teas pretty much alone. To bloom well, they must retain as much old wood as possible. Of course, dead and wispy growth should be removed and crowded centers opened up whenever necessary. Old Roses and Shrub Roses can be handled as you wish. You can cut them back to encourage low growth or, if you prefer, let them develop into large, free-flowering shrubs, as I do, with only an occasional removal of dead wood and little thinning.

From the large-flowered, once-blooming Climbers, like 'City of York', remove only nonproductive wood. Shorten last year's blooming laterals (side growths) to two or three eyes. Severely thin, or cut out completely, four-year or older wood. With everblooming climbers like 'New Dawn' and the Climbing Hybrid Teas, be sparing. Prune only enough to keep them in bounds and of presentable appearance. The older the wood, the better they repeat.

Finally apply a 2-to-3-inch mulch. Use shredded bark, wood chips, coarse compost, pine needles if you have them, but not peatmoss, which is dandy *in* the soil but not on top where it dries out and makes a crust that many rains will not penetrate but run off without reaching the soil. Water deeply in times of drought, but with a good mulch you will find that less watering will be needed.

Don't provide winter protection unless it is necessary. Find out how your neighbor handles his plants. Here no winter covering is necessary. True, we lose a plant or two now and then but consider this an opportunity for some newer replacements. Late in fall, we do cut back any long canes likely to be whipped around by wind.

If sub-zero temperatures occur and persist in your area, protect your roses by piling up about 8 inches of soil around each plant. Bring in soil for this hilling; don't draw it up from the bed or you will expose roots. And wait till there's a light freeze to do this; maybe this won't occur until December. However, if your winters are so severe that Climbers must be lifted down and covered with soil or straw, and Hybrid Teas require commercial cones or built-up shelters, I'd say skip roses. However, for *you* roses may be worth such an infinite amount of work.

The Pink Perfection Strain is handsome for July, the flowers suffused pink inside and out, but the plant does grow up to 6 feet and so requires staking.

10. *MOST LILIES ARE EASY*

Enchanting June-through-August Pictures

If you are among those who still think "lilies are difficult," do have another try. Most lilies are easy, unbelievably easy, and they don't disappear after a year or two. In fact, many kinds increase until the one bulb you bought becomes a great clump that all on its own makes a lovely garden accent.

The light on lilies broke on me some years ago when, needing color for an outdoor wedding in late June, a green time here that year, I put in fifty plants of the golden-orange Mid-Century Hybrid 'Joan Evans', each with one or two well-budded stalks. I outlined the Round Garden with them, planted them in front of an espaliered pyracantha, under the fringetree to welcome the guests, and with birches, hemlocks, and azaleas—the backdrop for the ceremony. These are all airy but not windy situations in sun or light open, not deep shade, with fertile soil and *good drainage*.

In two years, I could count seven to twelve stalks on every clump, not a bulb lost. What care did I give? In spring a scattering of all-purpose plant food, then a light compost mulch; in summer, an after-bloom foliar feeding with a soluble plant food and an occasional deep soaking if the season was dry—but no spraying. To keep the planting tidy, I cut off blooms but left stems—and for as long as possible—since nourishment is manufactured through the green leaves and next year's flowers depend on what the bulbs store up from them. When leaves turn yellow, stems can be cut to the ground.

Once I was lily-conscious, I planned a May-through-August pageant, with emphasis on July when most gardens need a colorful lift. The chosen ones proved of carefree nature. The lily bulbs with roots that we buy today, especially those propagated in this country, are just that—sturdy, healthy, and no longer virus-prone. With catalogues so glamorous, it is difficult to set limits but I have tried. Here are some reliable favorites for an enchanting spring-through-summer procession. I used to try to stretch the lily season into October by planting the Formosa lily, *L. formosanum,* with its white Easter-lily form and fragrance. In itself it was a handsome finale, but by fall it looked lonely there in the Apple-Tree Garden; also it reached 6 feet and needed strong support. To avoid staking, emphasis here is on lilies that do not grow much above 4 feet.

Lily flowers vary considerably in form as well as color, and plants vary considerably in height from 2 feet or less to 6 feet. Before you select, become aware of the various forms. The regal lily is a trumpet form; the Easter lily of the florist is the most familiar one. 'Limelight', also a trumpet, has pendent blooms; the speciosums and their hybrids have recurved petals and the flowers sway like earrings on supple stems; blooms of the Magic Pink Strain, Oriental Hybrids, open wide to form a bowl; Golden Chalice Hybrids are outward-facing; 'Enchantment' is upward-facing, less graceful, it seems to me. The Sunburst Hybrids like 'Bright Star' have pointed petals. Many of the Oriental Hybrids, as the three Imperials, produce very large flat blooms and some of these have slightly twisted or ruffled petals.

Four Thoughts

If you keep your Easter-lily gift plant growing indoors until the weather warms up in May, you can plant it outdoors in a sunny place, and you will almost surely get September flowers the same year.

You can cut lilies in bud and bloom and store them in a refrigerator set at the warmest temperature without defrosting. Then you

'Enchantment', one of the most reliable of garden lilies, opens vibrant orange, outward-facing flowers on 3- to 4-foot stems in June and July. Sturdy clumps like this are not long in developing.

can produce them for a party at home or a flower show. Take care not to store them too cold; excessive cold will damage the flowers; the leaves may darken first.

You can start a nice new crop of lilies by peeling off some scales from a big underground bulb. Planted in good soil and watered, each scale will produce a plant in one year, and some scales may produce flowering plants in two years.

Pink speciosum lilies with ferns make a lovely garden setting for a pan figure with impatiens and petunias at the base. Both pink and white speciosums are reliable and long-lasting.

If moles and mice are a problem, you may have to resort to chlordane to save your bulbs. While regular use of chlordane in the garden is not recommended, it will rid a limited area, like an established border, of the grubs that attract moles and the mice that use their runs. Mice can wreck a large lily planting in one season, as many have found to their sorrow. To use chlordane, pull back the heavy mulch in the border, apply the chlordane in recommended solution, and replace the mulch. The next year, in very earliest spring, repeat the treatment. Of course, discontinue the use of chlordane once the border is grubfree.

Late May–June

Coral lily, *Lilium pumilum* (*L. tenuifolium*), 24-to-30-inch graceful species with small, nodding, recurved, fragrant scarlet flowers for dry or sunny places, looks right in rock and wild gardens, and blooms in one year from spring-sown seed. It has a delicate air.

Golden Chalice Hybrids, with bowl-shaped, outward-facing blooms, in lemon-yellow to rich apricot shades; 2 to 3 feet, lovely with mists of gypsophila, white astilbes, and blue anchusa.

Mid to Late June

Madonna lily, *L. candidum,* glistening white trumpets, delightfully fragrant, on 3-to-4-foot stalks; set with only an inch or so of soil above the bulb—this one is not stem rooting—so must be planted shallow in September (or earlier if you can get bulbs) in light open shade in soil mixed with lime and wood ashes to make it sweet. The sooner these are planted, the better. The madonnas are prettier with the low-growing blue delphiniums, the pale 'Belladonna' or darker 'Bellamosum', than with the giant hybrid delphiniums.

L. martagon album, drooping waxen turkscap flowers in pyramidal clusters; in mid-June up to 3 feet; in open shade these come to stay. Nice for the wild garden. Plant 3 to 4 inches deep to top of bulb.

Mid-Century Hybrids, spectacular and sturdy, but not fragrant, in rich yellows to burnished red for late June on; in this group the brown-spotted yellow 'Destiny', light red 'Enchantment', golden 'Joan Evans', and lemon-yellow 'Prosperity', 3 to 4 feet, are enduring and indispensable. Good for your first try; these hybrids propagate freely. 'Paprika', a dark red, is also good and extends the color range. It and 'Prosperity' are outward-facing, others upward.

July

'Connecticut Yankee', early July, flaring salmon blooms in an airy head, followed by secondary and tertiary flowers that prolong the colorful period; 4 feet with heavy thick stems that are self-supporting; increases freely; many awards, outstanding.

'Magic Pink' Strain, delicate seashell, bowl-shaped flowers for June; unusually early for an auratum hybrid; 3 to 4 feet.

Regal lily, *L. regale,* white outfacing trumpets with yellow-flushed centers, deep pink to lilac outside, spicily fragrant, 3 to 4 feet; 'Royal Gold', a yellow form; both fine accents for July borders.

'Limelight', fragrant chartreuse, 4 feet, utterly beautiful, and a great favorite with everybody, including landscape architects.

'Moonlight Strain', big trumpets in shades of chartreuse and lemon-yellow; 4-foot plants; for late July. This and 'Limelight' are Aurelian Hybrids.

'Pink Dawn', a *L. speciosum-auratum* hybrid, lovely soft pink for July into August; useful where a 2-foot lily is effective.

'Nutmegger', late July, great candelabras of black-spotted, lemon-yellow flowers on heavy, 5-foot stems that need no support unless the site is windy; increases freely, underground and also from stem bulblets; a show-stopper, and a "sister" of 'Connecticut Yankee'.

'Bright Star', late July–August, a flaring bloom with creamy white, pointed petals zoned apricot; 3 feet; nice for a corsage.

August–September

'Allegra', elegant pure white and ruffled, very large with fine substance for August, an outstanding auratum hybrid; 4 to 5 feet.

L. auratum platyphyllum, Goldband lily of Japan, with flaring, white, gold-ribbed chalices, lightly spotted crimson, and a heavy-carrying scent; 4 to 5 feet; attractive with hardy asters, among the hardiest and most disease-resistant if American grown; endures extreme cold.

Imperial Gold Strain, huge, outfacing crimson-spotted white flowers with golden rays. Imperial Silver Strain, the same without rays. Imperial Crimson Strain, dark glowing red. All August, 4 to 5 feet.

L. speciosum album 'White Champion', pure white, with recurved petals, 3 to 4 feet, speciosums are most dependable for late-summer flowers; this one blooms into September; very fine and vigorous.

L. speciosum rubrum, called the "true pink lily," recurved and dainty, pink to blending red, sweet-scented, 3 to 4 feet; indestructible here with midday shade, handsome against evergreen backgrounds.

About Planting

Except for bulbs of the madonna lily, which are available in August or early September, you cannot obtain most of them before October or November, because they mature late. Then planting can be rather cold and difficult work I've found, especially if the ground has begun to freeze. To ease the task, dig the holes and prepare the soil earlier; fill up the holes with dry leaves and cover the loose soil with more leaves. Then it will be possible to plant with a trowel not a spade. Be sure to work in plenty of humus, bonemeal, and some sand to promote drainage, for good drainage is absolutely essential. Lingering water is fatal. Raised beds insure against this.

Some lily specialists, like Blackthorne Gardens, will store your order of bulbs under ideal conditions until spring, then send them to you at the earliest possible planting time. This is much easier planting, and very little growing time is lost. Indeed, Blackthorne recommends this procedure.

Set the bulbs 4 to 8 inches deep, measuring from the base, not the top. Stem-rooting (except the madonnas, the martagons, and some others not mentioned here), they need the long roots and support of the underground stems. If a lily grows only 2 feet tall, like 'Pink Dawn', the 4-inch depth suffices; if you select 6-footers—I avoid lilies above 5 feet, unless they are famous for stalwart stems—go deep so as to set bulbs with bases 8 inches down. Hard work, but your autumn shivers will pay off in summer pleasure, and once agreeably situated, lilies will stay by you for years.

11. *VINES*
The Plants That Wander

Whenever I hear the nurseryman's slogan, "it's not a home until it's planted," I want to add "—with vines," for surely there is no quicker or more charming way to relate a house to the land or to give it a homelike appearance than to adorn it with suitable vines. Well-chosen vines, properly pruned, enhance architectural lines and many offer flowers and fragrance closeby for your pleasure.

Wisteria—It Climbs to Conquer

Vines have always fascinated me, and in the few times I have moved to a new house I have always provided first for suitable quarters for a Chinese wisteria, *W. sinensis;* and "quarters" are what are required. The growth possibilities of this vine are frightening. A Chinese wisteria can cover 200 square feet, pry up your shingles, choke your gutters, and loosen your shutters. This vine rises skyward by strong turning stems and means business every foot of the way. It does not belong on a small trellis or even on a small house, unless you are prepared to deal with it regularly. I am; I love it. I'd hate to go through May without a glimpse of those dripping lavender panicles, fragrant and bee-inviting, that hang below the arbor crossbars in the sun before the bronzy leaves unfold. But I wouldn't care to leave my wisteria to its own devices for a couple of years and expect to be able to locate my cottage under the fierce mound of growth when I returned. Actually, wisterias need attention from the word go.

Early on at Stony Brook Cottage I had an arbor built the length of the house on the east. Here the trained and established wisteria is far more decorative than awnings—and hardly more trouble—and, being deciduous, lets in the welcome winter sunshine for the window plants. To enjoy wisteria, first be certain to buy a flowering specimen, lavender or white, though the white has been less prolific for me. Now that growers offer vines in pots or cans, plants are safely moved in bloom and can be so selected at your nursery, or you can get a *grafted* plant by mail from a firm that *guarantees* flowers. Seedlings take seven years or more to bloom, and all that business about root pruning a stubborn specimen seldom works. If your patience is

Wisteria covers the arbor, clematis vines climb the pillars, and houseplants in hanging containers are suspended from the eaves. The east bedrooms are comfortably shaded from strong summer sun by the well-pruned deciduous wisteria that later admits the winter sun. Below, shiny English ivy, shaded by the vine, grows luxuriantly in an area where grass was a failure. The hose rack is transferred to the cellar along with the hose for winter storage.

not rewarded by flowers the second spring, discard the plant and start over.

Since residence will otherwise be permanent, select a sunny location and dig a big generous hole and fill it with good soil from your compost pile. Cut the young specimen back to six or seven joints and allow only one or two leaders to remain. Tie these to a support. When the plant reaches the top of the post, spread out the branches and tie them where you want them, or tack wire over a framework and the wisteria tendrils, believe me, will find their way. Remove sprouts regularly from base and trunk.

Through summer I like to thin out the green spread of lateral growth a little to let light through to the house. When flowering is well past, it's time to prune heavily, to climb up and cut back the ambitious tendrils to two leaf buds. This pruning is repeated about every three weeks until September. After that do only what must be done to prevent takeover. Pruning after late August removes too much flowering wood. A dose of bonemeal in fall after growth stops is a good thing and superphosphate in spring promotes bloom. You can apply superphosphate alone or use a general fertilizer high in phosphorus, as a 5-10-5 (phosphorus is the second number). Do water deeply in times of summer drought.

Clematis

The other posts of my arbor support clematis vines, and I prefer those with single flowers. The young, deep pink, May–June *C. montana rubens* in due course must fight it out with the wisteria, coming up at the other end, so that both can spread over the top of the arbor. This clematis grows quite quickly to 20 feet and in Philadelphia covered my big backdoor arbor by itself.

On the center post the regal blue-violet 'Ramona' enchants us all. It climbs the 8-foot post, spreads over the top a foot or so, and is richly decked in June with exquisite saucer-shaped blooms that give pleasure to guests in the bedroom beside them. A few blooms appear through the summer, and there's a nice display again in September and up to frost. The flowers are lovely to float in a bowl or combine in late fall with a "permanent" centerpiece of ivy clippings. Here the fat buds slowly open to flowers paler than those outdoors. If you are going to have just one clematis, I'd say it should be 'Ramona'. It's the one I always give to new home-owners.

Past the arbor and beside the breakfast casement, I have trained the white, dark-centered 'Henryi' so that some of the intermittent June-to-September blooms open at the sill line and others above at the top. Taping a few flower stems assures visibility from the breakfast table. 'Henryi' grows only to about 8 feet and suits this location perfectly; I do recommend it for mealtime pleasure. At the other casement corner, and flowering about the same time, the lavender 'Mrs. Cholmondeley' with long, pointed petals takes her parallel upward way.

Around the corner and running along the north kitchen casement and over the doorstep garden, the lilac-rose 'Mme. Baron Veillard' opens late in July. In warm October weeks, it still gracefully sprays mauve blooms above the small St. Francis statue there.

The species, *C. paniculata,* with its small, white, hawthorn-scented flowers and billowing masses of feathery seedpods was to have brought September scent and bloom to the north arbor built over the garage entrance. It grew 25 feet even through a summer drought but the heavy shade cast there by the old apple tree defeated it, and me, for there was little bloom. If you have a big sunny space for it, do plant this species; its end-of-season beauty and fragrance will delight you. A more successful choice for my northern shaded situation would have been the purple *C.* X *jackmanii,* a white or pink *C. montana,* or the handsome, striped, mauve May–June 'Nellie Moser', so dear to English gardeners.

For success with clematis, dig a decent hole, say two spade lengths deep at the most or about 16 inches—"half an hour's preparation for each vine," one specialist advises "because clematis are voracious feeders and will be expected to grace their positions for many years undisturbed." Work in some compost and plenty of lime; this vine likes a sweet soil. Then set each plant with the crown 2 to 3 inches below the surface of the soil. Give an application of lime in spring if you have a somewhat acid soil like mine and work in wood ashes saved from your fireplace, along with a generous trowelful of an organic plant food. If you have the strength, feed again in July and August. In the fall, sprinkle bonemeal and mulch lightly.

Plant clematis so that roots are in the shade but tops can spread out to get five to six hours of sun. An eastern exposure is fine here where I set plants on the *inside* of the arbor posts so that roots are shaded. If your plants are in a sunny open place, prop shingles over the roots or let pansies or verbenas grow close enough to shade them,

The pink anemone clematis blooming May to June grows quickly to 20 feet, an excellent vine to plant for concealment or, as here, for ornament.

and spread a mulch to keep roots cool. Do remember to water. Clematis needs a lot of moisture. Any summer week you don't have a heavy rain, lay a slow-running hose beside each plant for half an hour of soaking.

I certainly find clematis easy. My vines don't "get things," and I enjoy pruning and training these near-at-hand plants. I tie the developing growth around the posts with soft twine when branches are not stapled to the house. Driving nails into clapboards is terrible, the painter tells me, but I figure the walls will last as long as I do and the next owner, if he doesn't share my passion for vines, can have a big putty job done. I like Francis Wall Nails that have a pliable hook but these nails will rust, so are painted white like the house. Since clematis climbs by leaf stems, strips of 12-inch chicken wire offer a less troublesome, though less attractive, means of support than random fastening with nails.

Timing and Method of Pruning depend on the particular ancestry of the clematis you are growing. However, all new plants should be cut back to 12 inches, and the tips of growing shoots pinched out through the first spring and summer to induce branching.

Hard Yearly Pruning is advisable for the Jackmanii and Viticella groups, the kinds that produce June-to-fall masses of medium-sized flowers on *young* wood. In February, cut these down to 1 to 2 feet or lower:

'Comtesse de Bouchard'
'Ernest Markham'
'Hagley Hybrid'
'Lady Betty Balfour'
C. X *jackmanii*
'Mme. Baron Veillard'
'Mme. Édouard André'
'Ville de Lyon' (or leave this unpruned; it also sets blooms on old wood.)

Little Pruning is necessary for Florida and Patens groups that produce their large flowers through spring and early summer on *last year's wood;* late in summer in some seasons they also offer smaller flowers on young wood. Doubles belong to the Florida group.

'Belle of Woking'
'Duchess of Edinburgh'
'Nellie Moser'
'The President'

Prune Lightly or Hard According to Your Purpose. To get early and very large flowers, only thin out weak and dead wood in February. If you prefer a mass of smaller flowers late in summer, prune hard in February as for the Jackmanii group.

'Henryi'
'Mrs. Cholmondeley'
'Prins Hendrik'
'Ramona'

The wonderful rampant species and their varieties need little pruning except to keep them under control. In February have a look at the late bloomers like *C. paniculata,* and prune as indicated. Usually you will want to cut back stems to the base of last year's growth. Whatever control *C. montana* and its varieties require, as light thinning, should be attended to in winter.

If you don't know which clematis you have, don't prune for a year but notice *when* flowers appear and on *what growth* they occur—on new summer branches or on older woody pieces. Then you will know how to proceed. Certainly don't cut back any clematis severely until you are sure.

Four More Vines for Flowers

At least four other flowering vines are worth considering. The climbing *Hydrangea anomala petiolaris* is choice. It clings by root-like holdfasts with occasional nailed assistance from me to make it grow beside but not across the west casement of the plant room. With little sunshine, the great, flat, white blooms open in abundance late in June, but it took the plant two years to get going. Now the 75-foot possibility is obvious so I prune drastically to keep my plant ornamental. If you have a tall dead tree you'd like to cover, this would be a good choice.

The old-fashioned rampant honeysuckle *Lonicera halliana* grows wild around here, an invasive pest on my back hill where it must be drastically *mowed* once a year if anything else is to live there. But what about the superb fragrance of those buff summer flowers? I know it's June when the scent drifts toward the house, drenching my world with its sweetness. 'Goldflame', a night-fragrant, everblooming cultivar with showy clusters from May to frost can be safely introduced to limited quarters, being neither a straggler nor invasive like Hall's. This is a good choice for a lover of honeysuckle who hasn't all the room in the world to give it.

The trumpet-vine, *Campsis* (*Bignonia*) *radicans,* is another mighty grower for a sunny place. It fastens itself with holdfasts, and throughout the summer opens the handsome trumpets. 'Mme. Galen' bears clusters of orange-tinted blooms, and this rather than the species plant is the one to cover a fence, tree, or wall quite quickly.

The powerful silverlace-vine, *Polygonum auberti,* thinks nothing of traveling 30 feet quite quickly in the sun, a little more slowly though still determinedly in a north or western location as I had it. There I enjoyed its fragrant August sprays foaming up a trellis by the dining room and over the unsightly, black composition roof under my study window. In time, however, it proved too much for me; it was difficult to manage the growth over the roof (now covered by more attractive wood shingles) and its numerous progeny seeded like weeds through the laurel at the base. This was a poor location for a take-over vine that had been a lovely sight at another house where an

The powerful silverlace-vine is rampant, to be used only for extensive coverage; traveling quickly in the sun to 30 feet or more, it brings August scent and bloom high up, even to the top of this house.

extensive arbor had been at its disposal. For a long chain or post-and-rail fence or to conceal some structure you don't care to see like a broken-down outbuilding, this woody silverlace-vine gives fine coverage, but it doesn't belong next your house wall.

Rampant Foliage Vines

Along my New England stone fences and the upper brook bank, the native five-leaved Virginia-creeper or woodbine, *Parthenocissus quinquefolia,* has volunteered. So has poison-ivy, but it has three leaflets not five and turns just as glorious a scarlet in the fall. Since I don't "take" poison-ivy, I horrify the garden boys who do by pulling it out with an ungloved hand and now I seem to be rid of it. The Virginia-creeper is a rampant, deciduous woody vine handsome in fall and other seasons with small blue-black berries that the birds dote on. It will cling to a trellis with its own tendrils but needs a heavy one, will cover a fence or make an excellent groundcover for a wild area in sun or shade.

The so-called Boston-ivy, *P. tricuspidata,* is not native, does have three-lobed leaves and the same fine autumn tints. It is a deciduous vine for the city, clinging readily to stonework and growing to the top of two- and three-story houses in just a few years. It's not for planting against wood.

The fiveleaf akebia, *A. quinata,* is carefree and fast-growing to 20 feet in sun or shade, with small fragrant flowers in April. Akebia is nice if you want a screen "like a mosaic of maidenhair fern" or covering for fence or stumps but too rampant for a limited trellis. It is best isolated, for its underground runners are ubiquitous, and aboveground it can throttle a shrub or small tree.

For Bright Berries

For colorful autumn berries, there is bittersweet, *Celastrus scandens,* another volunteer that I use here for high dense hedging along the driveway. From my study window, I also see it next door clambering to the top of a tall deciduous tree where a fine yellow-orange autumn display gleams through early winter next a golden larch sparkling with needles. Male and female vines of the native American bittersweet must both be planted to get fruit. For the garden or a limited situation, avoid this rampant grower, which can choke to death less vigorous plants, and plant instead the Chinese bittersweet, *C. loesneri,* which is a "sure fruiter" on one vine. Either species provides the flower arranger with fine winter decoration.

Firethorn, *Pyracantha coccinea* 'Lalandi', is a shrub that can be handled as a vine, and surely no plant in fruit is more vividly colorful in fall and early winter. The large berries, which follow the conspicuous trusses of white spring flowers, are a glowing orange-scarlet. Evergreen in sheltered, sunny locations and requiring support, firethorn is beautiful espaliered or trained and pruned on a trellis. It will not thrive, as I discovered, in a shaded northern location. A form with deep orange-yellow berries is available.

Evergreen Climbers

English ivy, *Hedera helix,* glossy and clinging with its own rootlike supports, is a handsome evergreen but not for very cold climates. It will not grow luxuriantly much north of New York City, except in sheltered locations. I use it more as groundcover than vine, but for coverage of brick or stone walls, certainly not wood, which will rot beneath it, it hardly has an equal. However, keep it to northern or eastern exposures, for winter sunshine burns it. There are many varieties; I don't care for the variegateds except as houseplants, but the smaller-leaved Baltic ivy is attractive and hardier than the species. I have observed that with age the species changes character; leaves incline to lose their pointed outline and become smoothly oval. Small flowers and black fruits appear, and the vine becomes even more attractive, and more shrublike.

Euonymus has served me well in two places. I have planted and tied the bigleaf evergreen wintercreeper, with its spectacular red fruits to the shaded trellis at the back door, replacing the unhappy pyracantha there. This one has also suffered an identity crisis but is now properly called *E. fortunei vegetus.* Beside the brook, where a great stump reminded me of the demise of a once-beautiful elm and could not be removed because it concealed the garden light box, I set a sprig of the spreading euonymus species, *E. fortunei.* This must have been some five years ago. Now this splendid evergreen, here more vine than shrub, has mounded over the stump, and its numerous progeny grace the gardens of many friends. Extremely hardy, it requires nothing of me but summer pruning to keep it in bounds. To cover a wall or cling to a house, as I see it next door, the

Annual 'Heavenly Blue' morning-glories find strong support in the tall perennial growth of 'Henryi' clematis. These companion vines make a charming summer-long picture.

vigorous small-leaved *E. fortunei radicans,* a climber, with holdfasts is an excellent choice.

When you plant vines next a wall or post, set them out about a foot so roots can spread. This is particularly important for these rampant woody climbers. When you prune those that grow right on a wall, unless you wish to conceal something unsightly, let some of the brick or stone show through, thus breaking up the surface with areas of dark and light. Let your vines adorn rather than conceal. Study the effect you want, then be severe, completely removing some strong runners at their points of origin, and be sure you cut sharply there and leave no stubs. I wouldn't say these perennial vines are completely undemanding, but few plants can contribute more to the look of a home and the charm of a planted place.

Three Pretty Annual Vines

Bringing rare true blues to the garden are the morning glories, *Ipomoea,* with lovely 5-inch trumpets. There are pink ones too but with so many other pink flowers available, I always want just the blues. They are lovely for fence or trellis or threading through the thorny branches of a climbing rose. The variety 'Heavenly Blue' is choice with an "improved" strain coming into bloom earlier and blooming later, I am told.

Get a headstart by planting indoors early, though not until after the first of the year because seeds aren't likely to germinate sooner. With a sharp knife, nick the side of each big seed, soak overnight in warm water, and plant individually in 2-inch pots. You will have bloom in exactly eight weeks so a late February sowing is about right. If you want a few pots of delectable blues for your window, plant January first and you will have flowers by March.

Some years the cup-and-saucer vine or cathedral-bells, *Cobaea scandens,* with green-and-purple blooms is a nice addition. It grows tall to 30 feet in one season in sun or shade. Start it indoors about six weeks before after-frost outdoor planting.

The dainty, black-eyed-Susan-vine, *Thunbergia alata,* is another choice annual. All summer long, it produces pretty white, yellow, or orange blooms in sun or light shade, a graceful vine for a window-box; don't expect it to grow much more than 3 feet. Sow this one indoors in March or outdoors in May and water plants well in dry weather.

A freeform bed of Christmas ferns and white violets with an edging of blue myrtle flourishes here in shade, replacing a problem area of grass.

12. *GROUNDCOVERS*

Three Loves Have I and One Terrible Hate

Now let's consider groundcovers, indispensable for today's planted place. A couple of years ago, I took a good hard look at what was running me ragged here and I discovered it was those lawn areas where grass failed and had to be replanted year after year in many quite small, a few large, and one middle-sized area (like the three bears). Particularly where there were heavy tree roots, grass was impossible. I noted the thin stand in deep shade under the arbor to the east of the house, along the brook bank on the west, and in a curved section on the north.

My Three Loves

So I turned with confidence to my three loves, groundcovers, not rare, but tried and true, and all evergreen—the upright Japanese spurge, *Pachysandra terminalis;* the creeping, bright blue or white spring-blooming myrtle or periwinkle, *Vinca minor;* and the trailing English ivy, *Hedera helix,* the green not the variegated type. First, I outlined several freeform beds; then I swelled out existing plantings of groundcover so as to include meager edging stretches of grass. If you want to do this, first buy at the hardware store fifty or so 12-inch pointed stakes. Thrust these in to make your new outlines; then lay a pliable hose the length of the curve but don't dig for several days. Instead, study the new lines from several points of view outdoors and also from windows and doors inside. When you are satisfied that you have a graceful curve, go along the outline with a sharp edger and dig out the new sections.

If you have a compost pile, mix in compost before you put in new plantings. However, if you are extending a pachysandra bed, you don't have to be particular. Apparently this 8-to-12-inch plant will thrive under the most untoward conditions and in the poorest soil;

The scented sweet-woodruff, *Asperula ordorata,* the May-bowl herb, makes an excellent groundcover in sun or shade, flowering white in May and June. Here it flourishes below the rock with ferns along the Cliff Path of wood chips.

In light open shade white violets make a lovely ground cover in association with Christmas ferns and an edging of myrtle. Fitch photo.

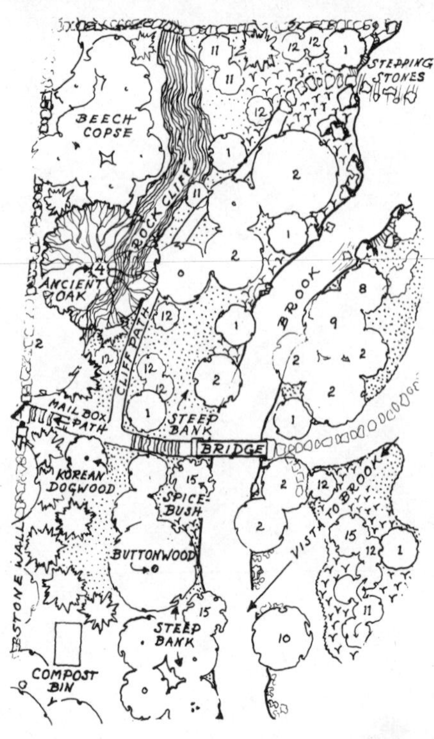

it just fills out faster in good soil. It thrives even in deep shade but will stand some sun. I pull up big sections from an old planting, cut roots back for easy handling, and just stick clumps or even clusters of unrooted pieces in the newly spaded soil. Eight inches apart for single plants is about right, and such plantings begin to fill out by the end of summer. Next a mulch is needed. I use pine needles because I *have* pine needles; wood chips, salt hay, but not grass clippings, will also serve. Unfailing attention to watering is essential for new plantings. If pachysandra dries out before it is established, it will wilt and not root and you'll have to replant with fresh pieces.

On the west slope under trees along the brook, a grassy green bank was long my foolish dream. It never came true in that shaded, root-ridden area. Now my second love, the April-flowering periwinkle, covers the bank. It is interplanted with the May-blooming, wild blue phlox, *P. divaricata.* These two make a colorful spring picture, far lovelier than the greenest greensward could be.

If you already have a large myrtle area, you can transplant good-sized clumps, setting them about 15 inches apart, and go on "myrtlizing" freely as I do. Perhaps there is an ancient graveyard close by where myrtle obviously is crowded; well, proceed as you see fit. Usually friends can spare you some plants. If you must buy plants, set the little sections fairly close, at about 8-inch intervals. For a good start in an area of heavy roots and poor soil, dig adequate holes for each and fill in with good soil or peatmoss. If you have compost, use that and spread more over the whole bed.

The first year with myrtle you will be busy-busy cultivating unless you spread a deep 3-to-4-inch mulch to keep down the weeds. I used wood chips the first year; buckwheat hulls also look nice, but both cost the earth for a large area. Coarse compost will also do. Attention to watering is vital. Plants competing with tree roots in shade need a great deal of water and food. Until it is established, I fertilize myrtle at the same time as the lawn, April and late August or early September, and with the same high-nitrogen material. The second year plants will be expanding; your watering, mulching, and fertilizing program will begin to pay off. The third year, "O frabjous day," as the father said to his son who slew the Jabberwock, your myrtle groundcover will be thick and practically self-sustaining, except that watering in times of drought is worth doing.

Although myrtle forms thick mats, early bulbs will thrive among them. In myrtle under a hawthorn, I planted the spring crocus, 'Mammoth Yellow', and early 'King Alfred' daffodils. You may prefer grape-hyacinths or wood-hyacinths, scillas, or snowdrops. Any of them look pretty popping up among the green mats.

English ivy, my third favorite, is a slow starter but when established, at least by the third year, it is mightier than the mightiest. Set 8-inch cuttings—there are roots along the stems—about 15 inches apart in a north or east location. Avoid exposure to winter sun, which usually burns it if the ground is dry. And you will be wise to keep ivy away from house foundations or else remember to clip sternly there, as I do repeatedly. In my experience, only wisteria has the same power to loosen stones and rip out shingles.

A well-established planting of glossy English ivy is a fine sight. I have it under the arbor, where grass refused to grow, and I edged the bed there with that handsome yellow hyacinth, 'City of Harlaam'. On the north I reduced another troublesome lawn area with a wide bed of English ivy. It fills a 3-foot space on one side of a flagstone path, but for the sake of a fluid line stretching from one end of the property to the other—and plainly seen beyond the Apple-Tree Garden—I retained the curved grass on the other side. This grass in a shaded northern location is naturally demanding, in need of more food and water than the rest of the lawn; I have a feeling its days are numbered and that more ivy is in the offing.

I have mentioned only a few of the areas where these three groundcovers serve me. Actually, there are many more. I put in pachysandra in any little prone-to-weeds spots I see, as a triangle on the garbage-box path, or around a specimen holly where weeding would be a chore. However, I don't let it or any other groundcover crowd shallow-rooted plants, like azaleas and rhododendrons, that require a mulch. I use myrtle as a clipped edging, like a low hedge, along walks and evergreen plantings, and to extend azalea beds under the big white birch where grass failed at the outer edge. English ivy is also doing an unexpectedly good job in a quite moist area in the Cliff Garden. Once you are aware of the small, as well as the larger, benefits of these dependable groundcovers, you too will be tucking them in odd places to save you work there.

Other Good Groundcovers

Of course, there are many, many more good groundcover plants; whole books are written about them. I am only giving you an account of mine.

I enjoy white violets in a bed of Christmas ferns and daffodils edged with myrtle. White violets are not quite so invasive as the blues, but they also are not backward about coming forward, and so lovely in bloom. I always feel as if they asked me, "Will you love us in the summer as you do in spring?" and I always answer, "Maybe." So far they're safe.

In the Cliff Garden, I have fine carpets of the Maybowl herb, sweet woodruff, that hardly grows above 8 inches. Plants are set 8 to 9 inches apart. The modest wild lily-of-the-valley appeared there on top of the rock. The garden lily-of-the-valley I plant only where there is some sun or quite light shade; it won't bloom at all in deep shade. Also I use it where I can control it or where its invasive character is an advantage.

The foam-flower, *Tiarella,* blooming white from April to July, is spreading out rather slowly in the Fern Garden, and the Christmas fern, *Polystichum acrostichoides,* is a fine tall groundcover there, growing to 30 inches. Plants double in size about every third year and can then be divided. I set small plants about 20 inches apart. For lightly shaded areas of woodland, goldenstar, *Chrysogonum,* is choice, colorful from April to June; I have also used it to edge other plantings.

For broad coverage on areas of the back hill, I like the sun-loving memorial rose, *Rosa wichuraiana,* dark green and lusty, with lovely fragrant white flowers. The hybrid 'Max Graf' is pink. Spread a thick mulch under either of these so you won't have to pull out weeds and grass from among the prickly branches.

On one bank of the brook the Virginia creeper or woodbine, *Parthenocissus quinquefolia,* volunteered service and was welcomed. It is an excellent, *rampant* groundcover, nice over stone walls, too, and turns a glowing red in fall. It is easy to lead along where you want it to go, and sometimes seems to grow about 3 feet a week.

A curving bed of New York ferns and pachysandra is a cool sight in summer, and will be extended still more to reduce the area of grass, which gets spotty here in shade and summer heat.

Three other covers I have planted but I like them less because they have not moved fast, perhaps because their situations here are not entirely favorable. The evergreen wintercreeper, *Euonymus fortunei vegetus,* is a handsome vine, useful for certain locations but not for the steep bank above the brook where it has been disappointingly slow. *Pachistima canbyi,* an attractive foot-high evergreen, is expensive to acquire, and it too has spread little in the three years I've had it on the brook bank. I appreciate both the low and tall epimediums, covered in May and June with lovely yellow, white, pink, or red flowers, but they haven't moved very fast for me either.

A friend of mine dotes on *Lamium maculatum,* the dead nettle, one of the mints that on her place has been most satisfactory. It comes with green or green-and-silver foliage and produces lavender

On the west, a pathway of steppingstones leads from the bridge to the screened-in terrace. In summer, myrtle and *Phlox divaricata* make a green bank covering, so much more satisfactory in this damp, shady place than the former poor stand of grass.

or white flowers all summer. These are not the greatest so she prunes plants low to avoid them. But lamium is a mighty creeper in sun or shade; and it will move helpfully into desolate areas to save your weeding there; it may also crash in where not wanted. I grow lamium as a houseplant and find the long strands can almost serve as window curtains.

Since I have no vast sunny areas of groundcovers, I recommend from observation not experience, the heat-and-drought-enduring native junipers, *Juniperus horizontalis* and its cultivars. The foliage is ferny, dark green or blue, sometimes with purple or wine tints in winter. To be sure of a color you like, try to see a collection in a nursery. 'Wiltonii' or 'Blue Rug' and 'Emerson', which is rather slow-growing, seldom exceed 12 inches. Steel-blue "Bar Harbor" may grow to 18 inches. Another fine prostrate juniper is *J. sabina tamariscifolia,* with bright green frondlike branches, a slow grower that may make mounds 18 inches or even 2 feet high in time, and will stand full sun.

The evergreen bearberry cotoneaster, *C. dammeri,* is excellent for moist soil and frequently roots along the stems. It doesn't grow above a foot and has a fine fall crop of red berries.

Now for my great hate. I would not wish on my worst enemy a single plant of that conscienceless invader, the stringy-rooted goutweed, *Aegopodium podagraria.* How it came to my fern garden, I'll never know. It's a vicious plant and even when one year, and one year only, I got rid of every evident scrap of it for one week, the next week it was its cheerful, competent, take-over self again. Literally, I hate this plant. For a road cutout, a barren waste, a clayey slope, I suppose it has use, but for anybody's garden, no! (I once told my granddaughter I didn't have strong-enough swear words for this plant; she advised attendance in the sixth grade at her school where I'd soon learn them, she promised.) Anyway I'm always on the watch for a stray goutweed moved with a transplanted fern, or carried along with other plants I am giving away, which has happened. Actually this ubiquitous devil seems to have wings for I keep finding it faraway from its evident place of origin, the Fern Garden.

I have a friend who once admired a stretch of flowering goutweed from a train window, and later with some effort secured plants from the railroad bank for a shady place in her small, meticulous garden. Now, ten years later, we commiserate yearly on the power of unwanted plants.

GROUNDCOVERS

For convenience, this list by common names.

NAME	HEIGHT IN INCHES	EVERGREEN OR DECIDUOUS	FOLIAGE, FRUIT, FLOWERS	CULTURE	REMARKS
Bearberry cotoneaster *C. dammeri*	12	E	Bright red berries.	Partial shade, moist soil.	May root along stems, good cover for banks.
Blue Phlox *P. divaricata*	8–12	D	Lavender or white.	Moist shaded areas.	May flowering, exquisite, spreads quickly.
Christmas Fern *Polystichum acrostichoides*	3	E	Swordlike fronds.	Partial shade; moist acid soil.	Wooded areas or in beds under trees.
Dead Nettle *Lamium maculatum*	6–8	D	Lavender or white.	Sun or shade; indestructible.	April–August flowers but better pruned off.
English Ivy *Hedera helix* *h. baltica*	6	E	Glossy dark (green) leaves. Small-leaved.	Light or deep shade.	Avoid winter sun; keep away from house foundations. Hardier than the type. Both spread fast.
Evergreen Wintercreeper *Euonymus fortunei* 'Coloratus'	Prostrate	E	Size and shape of leaves varies.	Shade or sun.	Rambling, not upright, for banks; purple winter tones.
Epimedium	8–12	E	Flowers, various colors.	Shade or sun; acid soil.	Colorful May–June flowers, choice, but slow to cover.
Foam-flower *Tiarella*	6–12	D	White flowers.	Partial shade, moist woods.	April–July.
Goldenstar *Chrysogonum virginianum*	6	D	Yellow flowers.	Partial shade, rich, moist soil.	April–June, wild garden, not reliably hardy, worth chancing.

Japanese Spurge, see Pachysandra					
Juniper *Juniperus horizontalis*				Sun, drought-resistant.	Select in nursery, many forms.
'Bar Harbor'	creeper	E	Steel-blue foliage.		
'Blue Rug'	prostrate	E	Blue.		Same as 'Wiltonii'.
'Douglasii'	prostrate	E	Blue.		Violet tones in winter.
'Emerson'	18	E	Blue.		Slow-growing.
procumbens 'Nana'	36	E	Blue-green.		Layered effect; most desirable.
sabina tamariscifolia	18	E	Bright green.		Will grow in sun.
Lily-of-the-valley *Convallaria majalis*	8	D	White flowers.	Open shade to part sun.	May–June; very fragrant.
Memorial Rose *Rosa wichuraiana*	trailing	Semi-E	White flowers.	Sun or light shade.	Late summer bloom; dependable for banks and slopes, roots where it touches.
'Max Graf'			Single pink.		
Myrtle *Vinca minor*	creeper	E	Blue or white.	Sun or shade.	Colorful and effective in late April, spreads fairly fast.
Pachistima canbyi	12–18	E	Prostrate shrub.	Sun or shade, acid soil.	Spreads slowly.
Pachysandra *P. terminalis*	8–12	E	Tiny white flowers, dark green foliage.	Shade to shifting sun; any soil.	Early May bloom, not showy, fast grower.
Sweet Woodruff *Asperula odorata*	8	D	White flowers, leaves in whorls of eight.	Moist shaded areas.	May–June, charming, blossoms used in May wine.
Virginia Creeper *Parthenocissus quinquefolia*	creeping	D	Small blue fruit.	Woody vine, rampant.	Brilliant scarlet in fall.

On the east, along the front of the house, a path of flagstones set in turf in a pattern first laid out on paper leads from the driveway around the corner to the front door. Stones are set low enough for the mower to pass over them; the first stone and the one at the corner are larger than the others.

13. PATHWAYS, DOORSTEPS, AND DOORYARDS

From Here to There with Pleasant Pauses

The path with an obvious direction strengthens a design; the path that turns and beckons toward an unknown terminus gives interest. I like paths of both kinds and have laid out a number of them here. Some facilitate traffic, one leads to a concealed garden; two to hidden compost arrangements. And one curving planted path constitutes a garden in itself. When you lay out *your* paths, take your time. Find out first where you want to go quickly and directly, and where you want to wander leisurely, perhaps to some hidden feature. Then mark paths tentatively before final decisions. The hilly terrain here with a sharp rise above the brook on the west and a slow but longer rise, actually a hill, on the east above the flat area surrounding the cottage makes many paths possible, and also essential.

Kinds of Paths

If your property is flat and oblong or square, you can make it much more interesting by laying a path along one or both sides and planting broad beds between path and property lines. I've seen this work out attractively inside a fence line. Sometimes a narrow path makes an attractive little garden where otherwise there would be only fill-in plants. I know such a 6-foot-wide area with an 18-inch path of steppingstones beside a lofty arborvitae hedge. You aren't suppose to walk there, only to look down into it from the side. A variety of ferns grows in abundance and there is a birdbath with a watchful owl—an imaginative use of a narrow space. Sometimes the paths themselves constitute a garden as in one I know based on the design of a conch shell and planted with herbs.

At Stony Brook Cottage the essential entrance path is a comfortable 54 inches wide, made of flagstones. The first stone is full width 18 by 54 inches, and the stone at the turning of the path is the same. The other two stones are about 18 inches square or 18 by 24 inches, all laid out in a design that was first worked out on paper. This path leads from the disembarking point of the driveway, along the side of the house, and then around a corner to the front door. A path laid out before the turn of the drive would have been more direct, perhaps more practical, but not so interesting.

The flagstones and the random stones of other paths are set low enough for the mower to pass over them but not so low that water collects or grass grows in to require constant clipping. Stones are first placed, then the outlines marked with a sharp edger and the patterned areas dug out the required 1 to 2 inches, depending on the thickness of the stones. Only the on-view flagstone entrance path gets a once-a-year clean-up clipping.

A practical path of random stones made from a great heap discarded when the open-to-bugs-and-sun terrace was made into a comfortable screened-in room follows the line from backdoor past garbage box to porch. It is joined by a graceful path that follows the edge of the myrtle-planted bank of the brook to the wooden footbridge. I sowed grass seed lightly but did not fertilize, for here in acidity and shade no-trouble moss develops and it looks just great. In a year or so more the feeble grass plants that served their interim purpose will be crowded out and the mower can skip this area entirely.

On the other side of the bridge a direct, practical path of stone steps leads straight to the mailbox but is bisected on the left by an indefinite grass path leading to the big wire-enclosed compost area and the hidden trash pile. This path is wide enough to accommodate a wheelbarrow. To the right the Cliff Path follows the other bank of the brook and leads down to steppingstones across the brook.

A path of flagstones, all of one size, leads from open lawn to the secluded Round Garden with borders of pachysandra on each side below masses of laurel.

When the water is low, you can walk across to another flight of stone steps that joins the brook path on the other bank.

The Cliff Path follows the slope of the land and is edged with a 1-by-4-inch furring strip (that's a pliable board!) secured by steel "hairpins" made by a blacksmith. These loop over the furring 4 inches on one side and are securely thrust deep enough into the soil to hold the furring, particularly on curves. An edging like this is most satisfactory, worth having made for paths that can be overwhelmed with leaves and too easily lose identity merging with the surrounding soil. A 3-inch-deep covering of wood chips makes a dandy

Here is a northwest view of the brook and bank path beneath a sugar maple. When the water is low, we can walk on broad, dry steppingstones across the brook from cliff side to house side. Krieg photo.

dry path. These chips are free for the carting in some towns from tree-service firms, but not here. Nothing is free where I live, but the wood chips last well and are worth some investment. First I used buckwheat hulls; they looked fine but disappeared too soon due to rain and wind, and they are expensive if a great quantity is needed.

A winding grass path can be charming, and is a good idea where lawn merges into an area of different character, a wild garden perhaps or a Fern Garden as here. The grass associates the two and has the advantage of easy maintenance, being mowed along with the rest of the lawn.

The most delightful path here—it is for my winter pleasure and not visible in summer—is a long transverse path on the back hill. It starts low from the open meadow, a plank seat marking the entrance, moves almost straight across to the left, turns gently, and moves up smartly on the right to the summit, where there is a seat for viewing Long Island Sound when the old apple trees—once this was an orchard—are no longer in leaf. In late fall and winter it gives form to the hill and makes a pattern I enjoy seeing from the house with the trees in silhouette, the mounds of laurel alongside in pleasing contrast.

Doorstep Gardens

Where paths terminate at doorways, I like small intimate plantings to enjoy as I come and go. As I have remarked, I do not care for "foundation plantings" with their stereotyped formality, for this is a country place. Perhaps these descriptions of two of my small entrance gardens will give you ideas for yours. At the kitchen door shaded by the apple tree, an evergreen bittersweet or wintercreeper, *Euonymus fortunei vegetus,* grows up the trellis. Then in the 2-by-9-foot bed, also held in place by furring and steel clips, I have hyacinths 'Delft Blue' with yellow pansies tucked among them in spring and replaced in summer with, in some years, coral-colored impatiens plants and a few white nicotianas (both bought in bloom). Impatiens in a deep color looks nice in shade against a white house and the flowering tobacco has a good scent. A few pachysandra clumps keep the planting tidy in winter. The bed becomes a little shrine with the placement of the small figure of St. Francis. The clematis, 'Mme. Baron Veillard," is trained under the window. This bed is terminated by a dwarf evergreen, *Pinus cembra,* the Swiss Stone Pine.

Beyond the dwarf pine, the walk leads to the front door past the big ivy planting edged with those glorious yellow hyacinths 'City of Harlaam' under the arbor. Round the corner to the right of the path the 9-by-12-foot front doorstep planting, edged with myrtle, is a long delight from early March, sometimes late February, depending on weather, when the winter honeysuckle bush, *Lonicera fragrantissima,* at the side opens tiny blooms of piercing sweetness, the scent noticeable, for almost two months. Beside it *Clematis montana rubens* climbs the arbor post and opens pink blooms in April.

Below is a bed of lilies-of-the-valley, fragrant in May and punctuated in July by clumps of the golden Mid-century lily 'Joan Evans'. In June the fringetree, which dominates the planting, perfumes the air and shades the doorway with its beautiful umbrella of foliage. To the left of the steps is a spreading yew for the winter picture and reaching from around the corner a *Viburnum carlesii* trained espalier fashion. It pins on coral brooches in May and its spicy fragrance delights every guest. In August I cut back the lilies-of-the-valley, now looking a bit rusty, to make room for pots of chrysanthemums. I set these out everywhere on top of the ground for color through the autumn weeks.

I think doorstep plantings should be personal and very special, plants you want to dwell on, since you see them daily, and with fragrance if possible. At one porch entrance I have lilacs, 'Hugo Koster' and 'Ludwig Spaeth', and two choice tree peonies, the glistening white 'Gessekai' (Kingdom of the Moon) and yellow 'L'Espérance', both lightly scented, with the lemon-yellow daylily 'Thistledown' for its pale evening beauty.

The other entrance is flanked by fragrant azaleas, *R. arborescens* and *R. viscosum* on the one side, pale pink mountain-laurel and green royal ferns on the other with blue *Scilla sibirica* and blue-flowering periwinkle for color and groundcover.

These then are *my* doorstep gardens. You can easily plan for something similar, knowing that little room and less care is required (if you mulch in summer), and that the rewards are great and also quite special. Maybe you will want only a small step garden. For this you could use double cement blocks as plant boxes. I saw a delightful pair of these filled to overflowing with bright red geraniums and pure white vining petunias, both growing in the soil that filled the holes in the blocks.

This brick-edged herb walk of New Jersey grit is 42 inches wide and leads from Lucy Sargent's terrace to an open field. On the right, the tall plume-poppy dominates, with spearmint, curly allium, and Italian thyme below; on the left, beebalm, speedwell, and Roman wormwood are edged with germander.

Dooryard Gardens of Herbs or Roses

Perhaps you can have something I've never managed, a *front* dooryard garden with a wall or fence, well contained, a whole garden close at hand for your pleasure, yet small enough for you to keep quite easily in practically perfect condition. Such a dooryard garden is a pleasant return to the Victorian way, I think, when people sat on front porches and had flowers out front to enjoy—and to share. In time, the front porch became passe. Entrances became formal and shut out the world. Stern green foundations prevailed.

Today it is again "permissible" for you to have a gay front yard, to *welcome* guests instead of *admitting* them, to share your garden with the passerby or, lacking garden space elsewhere, to develop there a garden room, but a *front* room. Perhaps you would like to plan a garden of herbs, as New Englanders often do, or a riot of bloom to charm the passerby.

If you are one of the herb enthusiasts—and those I know can hardly see other plants—you will enjoy a front dooryard garden or a "yarb patch" near your kitchen, always providing you have plenty of sun. Here will grow your favorite culinary herbs. One good cook I know considers indispensable at least a dozen, and I may say when she entertains her dishes are likely to be strongly herbal. Her dooryard garden includes basil (both sweet and bush), chervil, chives (including garlic chives), mints, parsley, rosemary, sage, tarragon for vinegars, thyme, oregano, and sweet marjoram.

Out of season she depends on commercial dried herbs but likes to use also the fresh herbs she has frozen in butter. For these, sweet butter is softened and finely chopped herbs worked in. The mixture is paddled into half-inch balls or pressed into carved wooden molds, firmed in the refrigerator, and then stored in well-marked pint-sized boxes in the freezer.

My particular pleasure is in the scented herbs that provide foliage or flowers for indoor arrangements or great jars to set on the summer porch. A dooryard garden of these might be edged with clipped Roman wormwood *Artemisia pontica,* dwarf lavender, germander, or santolina, either green or gray. It might include yellow and rosy achillea, fern-leaf tansy, cool cucumbery burnet and borage, spicy beebalm, lavender, blue salvia, old-fashioned garden heliotrope *Valeriana officinalis,* perhaps foxglove and rue, and two other artemisias, that is *A. abrotanum* and *A. absinthium,* and scented geraniums—to mention only "herbal-herbs." Of course, in the biblical sense all plants are herbs but we generally limit them to seed plants of soft or succulent growth, although rosemary and sage are shrubby and medlar trees have been included in herb gardens for centuries. Incidentally, call them "herbs" with an *h* or erbs without an *h*; you're all right either way.

Down the road from me there's a *shaded* dooryard in front of an old white saltbox. A New England stone fence surrounds it, interrupted by a hospitable white gate. Mountain-laurel, ivy, and pachysandra here are set off by various hostas and impatiens plants in melting shades of cream, lavender, pink, and salmon. Pink geraniums bloom in boxes set on a sunny section of the wall. How I enjoy this dooryard as I walk down the road for a breath of air. And what a generous expression it gives the house with its front-yard beauty open to all.

In the sun, of course, a dooryard can be a riot of color and fragrance. I remember a Philadelphia garden worked out with *choice* plants, the emphasis on roses, in a sequence of pictures enclosed by house and garage walls and a picket fence. Great care went into the initial preparation of beds to a 3-foot depth, and bloom there was magnificent in June and intermittent till frost. This garden was always pleasing. I have wandered through its 16-by-48-foot extent in all seasons. In winter, there was the attractive design of the flagstone walk, the neat beds, the pattern of the espaliered, red-berried pyracantha against the garage wall, with the climbing hydrangea and *Euonymus fortunei radicans* giving "a charming and flawless performance in this difficult exposure." There were the handsome greens of yew and holly, cherry-laurel, *Prunus laurocerasus,* and andromeda, with plants of *Mahonia aquifolium* espaliered against one wall, but some also growing naturally in a corner, and pachysandra planted along the house foundation to prevent muddy splashings.

In spring there were crocuses, hyacinths, tulips, daffodils, and pansies, the very beautiful Chinese redbud, *Cercis chinensis,* "far more lovely than the American counterpart" with heart-shaped leaves and lavender-pink blooms, and the cherry-laurel ablaze with white candles. I found this dooryard garden irresistible, even before the parade of roses, the summer frivolity of petunias and sweet-scented nicotiana, and the dramatic beauty of tuberous begonias.

The well-pruned fringetree has a fine silhouette in winter as it arches over the entrance to Stony Brook Cottage. Miner photo.

14. THE PRACTICE OF PRUNING

Why, When, and How

A certain amount of pruning—maybe only cutting back some peony foliage to let light into candytuft, more likely thinning out choked forsythia to promote bloom—is essential to the maintenance of a planted place. But proper pruning seems to be a great mystery though actually it's quite simple. To prune effectively you have to decide why you prune, when to prune, and how. One neighborhood joke is the spring pruning of a dwarf peach tree by a man who knows he should prune *sometime* but hasn't answered the why-when-how questions and so each year when he has the spring urge to do some gardening, he cuts off most of his forthcoming peach crop.

The Why of Pruning

The main reasons most of us prune are to keep plants in hand and to promote bloom. Clean open growth is also a means to health, and of course wind- or snow-damaged wood must always be removed. In my predominantly shaded place, I have to prune vigorously at least once a year to insure adequate light for shade-tolerant or even shade-preference plants. Here, if I let trees and shrubs go their lush way, there would hardly be a flower in sight. Comfort and good looks are also factors—and pleasant views and vistas.

I have a standing July appointment with my tree man for the big job. I can manage a certain amount of maintenance pruning myself but I am ladder-shy and wouldn't ever attempt the high pruning. However, with good tools, a man who knows his objectives can manage the business alone, except perhaps lofty tree work that requires professional know-how. Tree paint now available in aerosol cans is handy for tree wounds larger than a lead pencil, and much easier to apply than those messes we used to have to make up, stir, and spread. Pruning is fun and the results delightful, so long as you don't get carried away and chop and chop till nothing is left.

But about specific purposes. The fringetree at the front door is pruned high enough for a tall man to walk beneath without being conked by a low branch bent under rain or snow. Then certain branches are retained to give shade and privacy to the guest-room window and to cut off the sight of the TV antenna as you approach the door. A tree growing in a flower bed like my silverbell is carefully arched and shortened to let in light while an attractive shape is maintained and bloom increased through the reduction of wood.

The crab apples are thinned because I don't like ornamentals to look like blobs. It's a pleasure, particularly in winter, to see through the structure of a small or large tree. In fact, a properly pruned tree, freed of suckers at base and along branches, becomes a piece of outdoor sculpture. Such is my apple tree, its ancient trunk and limbs cleared to handsome advantage. Also the hawthorn planted close to the porch. Branches grow out horizontally and all below 8 feet have been removed so that, sitting on the porch, we can see through to the brook. Higher branches that tend to touch the roof by summer's end are cut back.

Behind the Round Garden is an old maple. It was discovered there after the elms, which were the original important backdrop of that garden, were removed because of the Dutch elm disease that took all of them here. I had the maple pruned to a bold form that made what was a haphazard tree into a handsome garden ornament.

Sitting on the porch, I come to various decisions. The great white birch has developed a drooping branch that obscures the path to the Round Garden; along the brook are two weedy trees that hide the

In my very first autumn here, the ancient apple tree, so much appreciated, was heavily pruned and it has had attention ever since in July to keep it in health and looks.

This 20-foot, double-pink crab apple that grew so unexpectedly tall beside the driveway is pruned to a pleasing open silhouette that sets off bloom and fruits. Left to itself, it was only a great blob in the landscape. Miner photo.

enchanting view of moving water; across the brook low branches of maple have grown in two years (since the last drastic attack) so as to impede the sight of the rock ledge. My *why* of pruning them is to remove this unwanted growth so as to keep open favorite garden vistas. Your *why* may be much the same but applied to different trees.

Once your new-planted big trees gain stature, they need little if any yearly pruning; nature mostly tends to what is necessary by discarding small dead limbs and twigs, and more effectively in some years than in others. However, in a hurricane wind, nature's pruning may go beyond your desire. It is in such a situation that you will be glad if you have tended to very old trees and freed them of any weak or rotten wood. A heavy branch falling on a roof can cause expensive damage. In any case limbs should never be allowed to arch over a roof unless frequently examined for safety, and certainly tree foliage should not touch a roof where it may cause rot through dampness.

With my oaks, maples, the balm-of-Gilead poplar, ash, and sweet-gum, little is now required because more than ten years ago decision was made on permissible height of the lowest branches and some were removed accordingly; the number of strong upper branches to be permitted on lawn trees was also determined, so the trees now have a limited number of heavy branches. The many white birch clumps are pruned to keep them open and see-through. All these notes add up to why I prune. Perhaps your *why* will involve severely cutting back trees like dogwood with branches that naturally sweep the ground. I don't cut all mine back but hand-clipping of grass is then necessary below but not every week because under shade, grass grows more slowly.

When to Prune

As for when to prune, with trees it doesn't matter much so long as you finish the job, say, six weeks before frost. Pruning stimulates and you don't want a lot of new growth that will be killed by frost.

Some plants seem to require constant attention. Wisteria is one and, if I didn't care so much for it and enjoy the way it shades the downstairs bedrooms on the east, I'd absolutely rip it out. Cutting back those ambitious strands of new growth at least four times a summer hardly suffices. A week after a severe July pruning, I measured new branches 5 feet long and waving in the wind. Then no matter how your vine looks, you can't cut back but only tie pieces in place

The winter honeysuckle, lovely in leaf, bloom, and silhouette, is pruned to a shapely 6 feet. The tiny white February-to-April flowers scent the whole east length of the house and the oval leaves hang on to November to catch the first snow.

in September or you won't have even a cluster of flowers next May. Big nuisance this, but a lovely plant. Clematis is much easier to cope with and the various named cultivars are truly beautiful. (In Chapter 11 the matter of vine pruning is discussed more fully.)

With flowering shrubs that need yearly attention, the rule is to prune soon after flowering so spring-blooming forsythia should be cleaned up early in summer and summer-flowering hibiscus in September. Actually all my shrubs are attended to at my tree man's convenience—and mine—in July. We follow the technique of removing a quarter to a third of tough old wood at the ground line every year with little cutting back of tops. Bobbed bushes look awful, and there is little need for bobbing if old wood is regularly removed. The amount of cutting back of branches that hang over driveway or lawn in July is so slight as to reduce bloom very little on the late shrubs. Old lilacs grown to roof height can be rejuvenated by removal of some of the ancient trunks at ground line if you wish, but I've been

Under the balm-of-Gilead tree, this big forsythia, regularly pruned to open growth, reveals its handsome fountain form, a delight to see from the house even before the branches are covered late in May with yellow stars. Krieg photo.

sorry I hacked mine back so much. They had a nice ancestral look before.

Some plants like the climbing hydrangea and *Viburnum carlesii* that I grow right against the house, nailing them in place regardless of paint, need frequent pruning through the growing season to keep them flat in the manner of espaliers, although I do not attempt formal espalier designs.

How to Prune

The detailed techniques of pruning are not the province of this book. Aside from advising you for your own work to acquire three first-quality tools—a hand-pruner, a lopper, and a pole pruner—combining hook and saw for not-too-heavy work—and keeping all three sharp—I'd urge you to read one of the excellent books on the subject, as Edwin Steffek's *Pruning Made Easy* or John P. Baumgardt's *How to Prune Almost Everything*. Either will give you shrub-by-shrub and tree-by-tree directions. Or, if you have a big planted place, do as I do and engage a professional for most of this important business of pruning.

A word of caution: Never allow anyone to prune the plants you love in your absence.

I have a definite "scream technique." I stand back from the job so as to determine what needs to go and what must stay and by voice and pantomime direct the man with lopper and saw. Not every personality could endure this but my pruning man, who knows every tree here—big and little—doesn't mind, for he agrees with me that pruning is an art and like me he enjoys practicing it.

15. *PROTECTION FOR THE PLANTED PLACE*

Thoughts on People's Pets, on Wild Animals, Pest and Disease

The lover of plants living in the country faces certain peculiar problems, some requiring unbelievable tact if his planted place is to survive amid alien forces. I've never had trouble with humans, children, and delivery boys tramping where you wish no paths. To them I suggest the back hill and driveway as alternate routes and explain why. They have always cooperated.

Concerning Dogs

Dogs are something else. Where I live devotion to them runs high. True, the local ordinance forbids their being on the loose, but what fond owners of a pet can bear to pen him up; what busy householder can find time to walk him? If a St. Bernard, collie, or Irish setter has ever rampaged through your lilies or, with cronies, made a winter path across your sodden lawn, you will appreciate my difficulties.

To check the pack travelers, I erected 6-foot-high wire barriers at their main entrances and exits, and these actually changed the patterns of their goings forth. Then I telephoned the owners of the larger dogs who understood my love of plants and provided more home life for their pets. Sympathetic and helpful also was the owner of a great water spaniel whose destruction of the mallards in the brook I could not endure.

Every year a delightful family appears in spring—drake, mother, and twelve or so fluffy bits that through summer develop into adorable young ducklings. Writing in my study, I look down upon their progress, as they learn to step over stones and logs bigger than they are. Fearless, the flock comes up on the lawn for a largesse of bread and crackers. But one year by September only the brown mother, four ducklings, and what I figured was the sister-in-law from their general attitude, came to me for food. I had already discovered the remains of the handsome mallard, and my grandson sorrowfully reported he had seen Jimmy, the water spaniel, drag down and drown two little ones. Of course, the dog was simply acting according to his nature, as both his owner and I agreed, and without rancor on my part, especially since with the spaniel restrained, the next year a full complement of ducks appeared in spring and swam safely and happily in Stony Brook all summer.

Now what to do about *barking* dogs that destroy the peace of my garden world as I weed or prune. I love silence and today there is so little of it—anywhere. In silence I like to hear the sounds of nature, not the mad howls (six hours by clock) of a penned-up dog being teased by a cat on the outside of his cage. The neighbor from whom I sought relief, explaining that I could neither work outside nor write inside under such stress, suggested I seek psychiatric help and she let her poodle go on barking for the regular stretch. Finally I called the police to stop a "nuisance." They did, and my neighbor no longer speaks to me.

Woodchucks

A small dog or so busy on affairs not involving digging or assembly is no problem. Indeed, I welcome Tommy, the little beagle, from next door who bays obligingly at the woodchucks, for to me the woodchuck is pure horror. My unfriendly point of view is not shared by all. To one gentle neighbor all manifestations of nature are sacrosanct. "Let the woodchucks come to me," she says, "I love them. The little ones are so cute." Patiently she adds to or subtracts from her plant lists; willingly, she restricts her choice by theirs.

Achillea, beebalm, coralbells, iris, peonies, and physostegia are not favored, but the specialties on the woodchuck menu are balloonflower, chrysanthemums (mine they ate to the nub), phlox, Oriental poppies, marigolds (which I should have expected to be too "strong"), petunias (but here I suspect rabbits), and zinnias. None of these can be safely grown in woodchuck land.

If you too claim your hard-won flowers as your own and not provender for scuttling woodchucks, what can you do? Shooting is both humane and effective. They are easy "to pot," according to my paper hanger who has offered to do the job here *when I am out.* I have never fired a gun myself, but once I borrowed one for an accommodating guest to use. Evidently my wise woodchucks got wind of trouble. Not until I returned the rifle to the owner *after ten days* did they appear again. As I drove back into the garage, Mr. Chuck climbed out a window areaway and made an obviously obscene gesture in my direction. And throughout that summer, he and his family continued in unmolested residence while I seethed.

If the woodchucks would stay on my hill, I'd willingly give it over to them. From the upstairs window, I see them cavorting there and growing fat to pony-size. But until recently they wouldn't stay put. One year they cut to the ground a whole bed of the lovely blue forget-me-not anchusa. But it was my Fern Garden that so fatally attracted them—and I mean fatally. I finally found a reliable means of dispatch via a fumigant, a gas cartridge, which is lighted and inserted in a burrow. To be successful, you must locate *all* the open ends of a burrow. After sundown, close all but one opening with soil and stones. Into the left-open end, insert the tube, the fuse lighted to dispense the gas. Then immediately close this opening with earth and stones. You measure results, and the possible need to repeat the operation, by the reappearance of openings next day, and of course the reappearance or not of the woodchucks. If the tunnels show use again, repeat the bombing. It is not easy to find all entrances and exits. Even if one is left open, too much gas can escape to make the dose lethal.

In the Fern Garden, where space is restricted and exploration for tunnel openings over the whole terrain is possible, the woodchucks have been ousted, but not, of course, from their lair on the adjacent property whence they come forth to dine on both fruit and plants in the Apple-Tree Garden. On the hill I know the population has only been decimated. However, I don't mind much if the woodchucks have learned their lesson and will stay up there—or else move on to the demesne of my hospitable friend.

My Resident Raccoon

Now about that truly beautiful and very cunning animal, the raccoon. Since I grow no vegetables, his presence outdoors was no problem. However, his intimate residence in my house was hardly agreeable. He got into the walls through an opening in the roof made by gnawing squirrels. Repairing the roof did not end his sojourn. For more than a week, he ran through these walls all night as I moved wildly from bedroom to bedroom, while the raccoon seemed to follow me. He even got inside into the storeroom, tearing out the insulation and *turning on the light* there by pulling the cord.

When he was out, as we thought during the day, we closed his new point of entrance, the vent in the eaves, with heavy wire, but he unbent the wire, as he had already unbent the aluminum louver, and continued going in and out of the house and rampaging through the walls. Finally we gassed him out by introducing strong camphor fumes from a vacuum cleaner into the partitions. To avoid the fumes, the raccoon—estimated to be more than two feet long and more than thirty pounds heavy—ran out through the vent we had opened for him. Now this is securely protected by a new metal louver with very heavy screening behind it, and he visits me no more.

Should a raccoon enter your peaceful country home, I can only recommend camphor. To protect your vegetables, especially corn, a fine stand of which a raccoon can destroy in a single night, set a live-animal trap, and later deliver the culprit to a local wildlife sanctuary, as I once did a baby skunk—with some trepidation, I may say.

Rabbits, Squirrels, Moles

Rabbits can be trapped the same way but their profiles, and their little ones, are so engaging I permit a certain *limited* population to remain for my entertainment. And squirrels are also here, for my bird feeders have always been made with squirrel guards and set beyond-the-jump distance from trees. A friend kept squirrels, also raccoons, from her feeders by smearing the posts with tanglefoot.

Sometimes squirrels get into attics. One man got rid of them by spreading camphor flakes over the floor and between the beams. Then he locked the place up to keep it safe from children. Another used a live-animal trap, caught the squirrels one by one and then released them far away. Unlike homing pigeons, I understand, they do not return to the scene of their depredations. If ever squirrels get into your house via rotting roof shingles, as they did here, don't think nailing up an opening with just any old board will keep them out. Their gnawing power is horrendous, so use a sound, heavy board, not a piece of thin plywood.

I have had no moles here but in other gardens I employed the conventional mole trap to get rid of them. Other gardeners have had success with chlordane scattered around the plants and inside the opened runs, watering the material in well.

Garden Controls and Clean-ups

Although I have been an enthusiastic gardener all my life, I claim no expertise in the matter of controls and cures. In fact, this is one horticultural area I have always tried to avoid—that of pests and diseases (their controls and their clean-ups). Since this place is much too big for me to handle anyway, I have put my trust in a Tree Service, the same one that does such a fine pruning job for me. Mindful of the ecological implications of every poison used, this Service has kept the many kinds of plants here in clean condition with minimal damage to birds, bees, and other wildlife. In fact, when it comes to birds, I'd say they are often their own worst enemies. I see the bluejays driving away the robins from the nests I have watched them build, the sparrows chasing the bluebirds from a house put up just for their benefit and after they had taken up residence.

Realizing that many home-owners would hardly have cause or wish to engage a service, I inquired of mine what the proper—minimal—procedures should be. I was given a very fine, large format, sixty-page manual to read, this published by the Extension Service of the State of Connecticut for the guidance of those in this grisly business. A *complete* manual it was, but I could understand only a little of it. After spending three hours on same, I began to crawl and itch all over; and my knowledge was advanced by a mere jot—first, I suppose because I have so little enthusiasm for the subject, and second, because I have never had even a whiff of chemistry.

Appealing then to my excellent Tree Service and to my wise County Agent for capsule information, I acquired these useful nuggets:

If you live where the gypsy moth caterpillar and elm spanworm or inchworm are practically epidemic, you can eliminate them with a dormant miscible or superior oil spray any time late in winter or early in spring when the temperature is above 45 degrees, and likely to stay so for forty-eight hours. Or you can wait till just before hatching time, about the first week in April, and clean up the egg cases; those of the gypsy moth are larger and more easily found than the smaller ones of the spanworm. Fasten a small paint brush to the end of a pole, dip the brush in creosote or creosote stain, and smear the eggs. This will destroy them. Or you can scrape them off and burn them; don't let them just lie on the ground or they will hatch and your trouble will be for nought. (Where I live, the town is making creosote available wholesale to residents, and the Boy Scouts are organized to do the job.)

After hatch period, if many caterpillars have escaped the egg treatment, you can tie burlap "skirts" around the tree trunks and dispatch the caterpillars that seek shelter underneath. (Ugh!) Or you can wrap a tight paper band or masking tape, smeared with "tanglefoot" around the tree and, in due course, clean off the trapped caterpillars—one of the gardener's less enjoyable chores.

The home-owner, if equipped with a hose-end bottle-type or a knapsack sprayer and a supply of a general-purpose mixture, can manage very well on his own. One neighbor sprays all his trees himself, even covering the top of his great pin oak, as he did during an inchworm epidemic. I am told you can control almost ninety percent of all likely trouble with three applications of an all-purpose insecticide-fungicide mixture—this for both pests and disease—if you spray at the right time and thoroughly cover those plants that experience has indicated are likely to need it—birches for leafminer, laurels for lacebug, hemlocks, pines, and spruces for mites. You will be wasting some spray material since you will often be attacking trouble that hasn't yet occurred or those enemies whose attacks are over, but you will enjoy considerable peace of mind. Also you will be spared delving into essentially gruesome matters. Your all-purpose mixture will probably include malathion or methoxyclor for pests and captan or ferbam for diseases.

Three-Point Schedule

April 15–May 1. The general-purpose spray will clean up the first batch of leafminers on the emerging leaves of birch, holly, etc., also overwintering aphids, mites, and scales, and borers on azaleas, dogwood, lilac, and rhododendron. Be sure to spray trunks well when you are after borers.

May 15 (or Mother's Day, not a nice association, but it seems that's how the Service remembers these things). Your general-purpose spray —we use Sevin here—will get rid of most leaf-feeding beetles and caterpillars, including those of the gypsy moth and the elm spanworm, lacebugs on andromeda, mountain-laurel, and other broadleafs; again leafminers on birch and holly, mealybugs, scale crawlers, leafhoppers, bagworms, sawfly larvae, and some aphids—a pretty collection of trouble indeed.

June 1. The all-purpose spray will tend to the continuing broods of the above creatures, also launch a lethal attack on gall mites, on psyllids (not necessary to pronounce the p), and white flies on andromeda, azaleas, boxwood, laurel, oaks, and pines.

Now should the summer be heavy with heat and humidity—the degrees on the thermometer and on the hydrometer (or the T.V. report) adding up to more than 150—everything will probably be attacked by a fungus disease—blackspot, leafspot, mildew, rust, and so on. At least one more spraying, this time with a fungicide alone, Fermate, Orthocide, or Phaltan, will be required on lilacs, roses, and lilies. You may notice that they are beginning to lose their probably already-spotted foliage. Your procedure now might be to apply one of the newer systemic fungicides and douse new growth with Benlate. This could even be applied in solution to the soil around plants instead of being sprayed on, but experiments are too recent to recommend exact amounts yet. The systemics have a residual effect that lasts for months. The poison is absorbed throughout the vascular system of the plant and all parts are now protected from the diseases that occur when heat and humidity soar.

These systemics with the long reach are a boon to the many plant-lovers who do not relish employing their leisure fiddling with sprays. Beside the fungicide systemics, there are insecticide systemics that can be introduced into the soil around a plant about May 1 at the rate indicated on the container, and watered in. As the roots get hold of the poison, they send it north to all parts. Even I can manage this kind of simple business—no mix, no mess, just lethal scattering of granules which are immediately covered with soil. For those who go in for birches—both the leafminers and I do—also hollies and boxwood, a systemic that will protect plants for a long period lets joy be unconfined. Furthermore, these soil systemics need not wait on weather or man's convenience but can be applied at any time the top soil is workable. I used the systemic Cygon on a big 'New Dawn' climbing rose and not only did it receive no unwanted visitors but there were no signs of disease either throughout the growing period. And this kind of double protection has been observed by other gardeners trying out systemics, although they are not yet advertised to deal with disease. Dr. John P. Baumgardt informs me that since systemics do not reach the nectaries of either flowers or fruits, they are not injurious to beneficial insects or wildlife.

So good luck to you and if this three- or four-fold control plan is too much for you, you can wait and see what horrors the season brings to your door and then apply proper measures, as unwilling communities had to here when the elm spanworm began to defoliate acreage and the subsequent white moths impeded vision. If you do wait to clean up rather than control, you mustn't mind too much if some damage has occurred ere you take your trusty sprayer in hand. In any case keep in mind that your County Agent is your best source of specific advice *for your area;* what I suggest here is general indeed.

In case you prefer to mix your own spray or be specific and apply the proper material for each situation, here is information I hope will hold at least until this book gets into print. The materials listed below appear in the manufacturer's statement of what's-what in his all-purpose spray. *Be sure to follow all directions* printed on the bottle or package—you may need a magnifying glass for the fine print. Where very small areas are to be treated, an aerosol can is a convenience. In any case, don't spray on a windy day. The names shown in parentheses are for *commercial* products.

Insecticides

Malation (Malathion) or methoxyclor (Marlate), a substitute for DDT, considered much safer. These are considered broad-spectrum pesticides for aphids, scales, leafminers, and mealybugs. Used alone, malathion gives protection for only three or four days; methoxyclor, a DDT relative but safer, protects for twelve to sixteen days. With either one you may have to repeat until the last batch of trouble has hatched.

Carbaryl (Sevin). For leaf-chewers, beetles, caterpillars, the gypsy-moth caterpillar, the elm spanworm. Here, we also got rid of the white butterfly stage of the elm spanworm with Sevin although I was told it would be impossible since they do not rest to feed and are so mobile.

Chlordane (Chlordane), long-lasting soil insecticide. For white grubs, black vine weevil, and chinch bug.

Dicofol (Kelthane), a specific for mites.

Lindane (Gamma BHC). For aphids, most gall insects, leafminers, lacebugs, borers, and lindane also has some miticidal properties.

Diazinon (Spectracide), a broad-spectrum material in granules for insertion in the soil to control chinch bugs, grubs; or as a wettable powder or emulsifiable liquid for a foliage spray.

Fungicides

Benomyl (Benlate), new systemic-fungicide spray, excellent *preventive* for blackspot and mildew on roses, and for diseases of groundcovers. Spray on new growth.

Captan (Orthocide) spray, dust, or soil drench for a broad range of diseases; this can be combined with most insecticides as a spray.

Folpet (Phaltan) an important control for powdery mildew and blackspot on roses. You will see it listed on the label of your all-purpose spray for roses and other flowers and fruit.

Good luck in this gruesome business. Keep your planted place cleaned up, removing spotted leaves, diseased stems, and faded flowers. Good sanitation goes a long way to help your chemical controls rid your garden of pests and diseases.

As for the big argument—to spray or not to spray—this must be *your* decision. I have yet to see a satisfactory pest-and-disease-free place where my favorite ornamentals were grown and no controls were used. My point of view is, of course, clear to you, although I am giving the praying mantis a chance in one bed of broadleafs. Here we try to keep the situation as a whole in mind and we proceed with care accordingly. I know that when an unexpected spanworm attack in this neighborhood made the outdoors impossible, Sevin restored livability. Even then some dedicated ecologists did not spray.

In a nearby town where spraying was done by only one home-owner, the birds at least approved his act. They flocked to his leafy trees away from the barren branches of the more ecologically minded. Who knows which was the better course? If your point-of-view is the opposite of mine and you can manage without dust, spray, or systemic, more power to you!

If you wish to pursue these matters in depth, turn to *Disease and Pests of Ornamental Plants* by P. P. Pirone, Ronald Press Co., New York, 1970.

THE VOICE OF EXPERIENCE

About Landscape Architects. They are indispensable. They have the training and experience to help you lay out your property—large or small—to the best advantage and usually at the lowest cost in terms of beauty and convenience. With a proper plan, you won't have to move trees that grew so fast and wide that they shut off pleasant vistas, or waste your money planting in ways that impede traffic, make outdoor entertaining difficult, or cut off light and air from the house. On the small property, they can create an illusion of distance by planting a strong foreground with a look-through effect.

Before I put in so much as a daisy here at Stony Brook Cottage, I sought expert advice, for I saw at once that if this place were to be satisfactorily developed, a proper, long-range plan was essential. Despite my many years' experience and my knowledge of plants, I knew I didn't have the designing skill required. First of all, the landscape architect laid out the walk beside the house, improved the poor curve of the driveway for better traffic and parking, and framed the house with a pair of crab apples planted at the edge of the drive. We chose fairly large specimens of sweetgum and ash for immediate shade. There we stopped until the bank balance filled up again. Through the years then, following the original basic plan, I have developed garden areas and carried out a great deal more planting.

A landscape architect can help you, as I was helped, to create beauty with convenience. Certainly few amateurs can manage the terracing of a slope or solve problems of grading. Good planning involves a private outdoor living space, play space for children, opening up of good views, closing off of poor ones, framing and shading the house, and screening a service area. Just as we go to the expert to learn skiing or golf, or even to get our hair done, we should go to the landscape architect for property planning. You can proceed in one of two ways:

Have a basic plan made with important features—walks, driveways, big trees—indicated for you to work on in due course. Or you can have the landscape architect plan and also direct a certain amount of the work at the start, perhaps advising you year by year, as the basic plan is carried out.

Fees are based on an hourly rate or an overall estimate for plan alone or plan plus supervision. The landscape architect with an accredited L.A. degree is not the same as the so-called Landscape Designer employed by a nurseryman to help you, with or without fee if you are buying a considerable number of plants. Here I must say that when I look at a newly planted place, with many trees and shrubs, there is rarely a doubt in my mind as to which kind of advice was secured. After all the expert *is* an expert!

Before this property was graded and planted, the advantages of the site were unknown even to the owners, Cynthia and Ben Luden, who took this picture for the record.

The landscape architect Eloise A. Ray produced this inviting entrance and livable terrace through imaginative planning, grading, and selection of suitable trees, shrubs, and vines. The owners augmented these with their own choice of perennials and bulbs. Miner photo.

However, all landscape architects do not work the same way. Some prefer large-scale parks and redevelopments; others enjoy small properties. Before you get involved, ask to see examples of work. Find out if the landscape architect you are considering is likely to take *your* tastes, *your* house, *your* property into consideration. Fitting a flat drawing-board scheme into a sloping site misses opportunities for interest with steps, walls, and outlooks. What you want is a creative designer who is willing to work *with* you.

Useful Property Measurements. It takes time but it's worth it to get fairly accurate measurements, particularly of lawn areas and extended shrub plantings. Until my wonderful garden helper, Kim, measured this place, pacing off some sections, using a long tape measure for others, I would stand stunned at the hardware store or nursery trying to interpret fertilizing labels for my situation, as 8 pounds recommended for 1000 square feet of lawn. The result was always one bag too few or one bag too much. Now I take a measurement memo with me and, allowing for the vagaries of my spreader, which cannot always be exactly calibrated for the selected plant food, I make out better; thus, north lawn 1200 square feet; south lawn 3200 square feet; driveway strip 1600 square feet, and so on.

How to Water, with the Supply Unlimited or Limited. No other maintenance factor contributes as much to the health and development of your plants, including your grass plants, as enough water, especially in periods of prolonged drought. Then *deep* watering is essential, not light sprinkling, which is worse than none since it encourages roots to grow toward the surface, where in time if no rain falls they suffer more from dryness and heat.

A good way to give plants a thorough soaking that will suffice for one to two weeks when there is no *heavy* rainfall is to place a very slow-running hose at the roots of each tree or shrub. I lay the hose nozzle on a shingle or board to diffuse the stream, and I don't move the hose on until there is actual puddling. To get water where the least does the most for trees or shrubs, you may find convenient a commercial "root feeder" attached to your hose. Thrust deep into the soil it makes every drop count. Or you can take a big juice can, punch holes in the bottom, and insert it a little beside a tree or shrub where the soil is soft enough to receive it. Let the hose run in this. As the can fills, water seeps deep into the soil. An inch of water a week is about right for lawns when there is no adequate rainfall and the temperature is above 70 degrees. You can measure what your sprinklers are supplying by setting a can under the outside drip and timing the inch fill. You will discover that not much is accomplished in half an hour.

One year of notable prolonged drought, I kept my lawn, especially the shaded area, in fine green condition all summer, and I lost only one and a half new shrubs from some fifty plants set out that spring. But it seemed to me I spent the whole summer moving hoses and sprinklers, and my water bill was horrendous. (The water company came to investigate, thinking that there was a big leak.) I know that one school does not believe in watering lawns, but prefers to let the bluegrass and fescues get brown because "they will come back after the fall rains." But that's not my school; I want a *green* setting for my house all summer and so the attention to watering. In the shade, if you neglect grass, it isn't so likely to brown as to disappear—and for good.

To reduce hose-dragging across the bridge to the Cliff Garden, I had an underwater section of hose set *in* the brook beneath some stones, then drawn up the hill to an extra pipe outlet with a faucet fastened against a tree. All summer I keep long lengths of hose ready on the path there. Unless you plan an automatic watering system (marvelous but expensive), do have a faucet on each side of your house and invest in yards and yards of hose. When the hose isn't in use, you can wind it up on removable brackets screwed onto the house wall. Readily available hose is a major convenience. In fall the brackets can be lifted off and moved for storage to other screwed-on locations in the cellar.

I like to watch the fan sprinklers that rise up and bow low as they deliver the welcome spray. I have both a Nelson Rainmaker and a Melnor Swingin' Spray, and also those metal rings that are so useful for watering under a big shrub or over a flower bed. If the pressure is kept low, loss by evaporation is slight and a considerable area can be watered before the next move. Sprinkler-watering is the easiest but also the most wasteful because of loss through evaporation as the fan of water is cast high in the air.

Early in the evening set the sprinklers in place for their *early* morning work. Then it's easy to turn the faucets on without getting feet wet running around in the wet grass. Pressure is likely to be high from 5:30 to 8:00 A.M. and the sun isn't strong enough to cause undue evaporation. As far as watering in full sunlight is concerned, it doesn't hurt plants. Nor is night watering generally harmful. You may have noticed that nature often waters at night. However, in hot humid weather night watering is to be avoided in certain locations because prolonged dampness of foliage is an invitation to bacterial attacks. Here, with so much shade and moisture from the brook, I never let the sprinklers go much after 5:00 P.M. Hoses running at roots cause no trouble at any time.

In some areas, an unlimited supply of water is not always available. Where city water does not reach and a well dare not be drained dry, water for plants must be carefully applied so that no drop is wasted. Avoid sprinkling in the heat of the day, when evaporation is fast; instead, water early in the morning and late in the afternoon and evening unless you too must ward against fungus trouble. When the water supply is very limited, and drought is apparently unlimited, some hard decisions must be made as to what plants to favor—probably the most valuable. That would mean trees, then shrubs, with the less costly perennials and annuals last, and the bluegrass and fescue lawn let go dormant in the hope of revival with fall rains. Needless to say, plenty of humus in the soil and a good mulch on top conserve moisture and reduce the need for artificial watering.

Treasure in Compost. In fall leaves produced on a shaded place like this are overwhelming to say the least, but what grand and unlimited compost they produce. And I do revel in rich compost. Certainly it's no problem whatever to acquire. I keep at least three big piles going simultaneously; these placed strategically for leaf hauling. Two measure 12 by 12 feet and are fenced with staked 4-foot lengths of 2-inch mesh wire; one side can be partly opened for unloading the wheelbarrow. When labor permits, these big piles are forked over about once a summer. A third smaller pile is less carefully managed, open for casual dumping. One pile is always decomposed enough for immediate use. I also have two slatted bins that I bought. Placed behind shrubs, these hold small amounts of fine stuff that decays quickly.

You know, of course, that on a small place you can conceal a good leaf pile behind a big forsythia bush and control it with a rampart of old boards. I've done that, too. And now I see there is a useful little compost kit available, fine for a small neat property; the bin is 30 inches high, 4 foot across of 8-gauge galvanized screening with two steel support posts. Compost-making tablets to give you about thirty valuable bushels come with the bin.

In the excellent News Letter published by our Connecticut Extension Service is another idea, Plastic Bag Composting:

"Line a trashcan with a plastic liner and throw in everything that would make good compost, as garbage [except where rats might be a nuisance]; organic materials except onions; leaves—intersperse or mix with other materials, don't use in large separate batches; grass clippings—treat like leaves, quantities of clippings become messy; and fertilizer—sprinkle a general-purpose fertilizer as leaves are added. (Omit diseased garden remains.) When the bag is full, add a quart of water, tie the top tight, and place the bag on the ground. When the second bag is full, place it on the ground and turn the first bag over. The first bag is ready to use after the fifth or sixth bag is filled."

Here at Stony Brook Cottage, the real gardeners, taking the grand tour with me, always admire the compost. I insist—and I do mean insist—that the piles be made with hollows in the center to catch and hold water, which speeds decomposition. And sometimes I place a slow-running hose for hours in a depression. Now *you* can be fancier and faster, using an activating agent in the compost and arrange, sandwich-fashion, layers of leaves, weeds, vegetable tops, even garbage, with layers of soil. But piles of leaves and grass clippings and green plant tops (try to keep out woody pieces if you can), left alone, eventually make fine, rich compost.

Emphasis on Spring Bulbs. You can't have too many spring bulbs. Along with shrubs they are the most rewarding of anything you can select for your planted place. From the late February or early March winter aconites to the end of the May wood-hyacinths and tulips, bulbs offer bloom through the months when colorful flowers mean so much to our winter-weary souls.

All these spring bulbs are of easiest culture. Most require light during winter and spring but accept shade afterwards when they are dormant. Thus, they prosper under deciduous trees provided these are deep-rooted like the apple, most oaks, sweetgum, ash, tulip-tree, and zelkovia, and many of the smaller flowering trees. They can't perform well if they must compete with a tangle of surface roots like those of Norway maple, horse-chestnut, poplar, willow, or European beech, and bulbs fade out in the deep shade of evergreens. However, most bulbs will accept the shadow of buildings if there is light from open sky above but not tulips; they need full sun.

All bulbs require good drainage and a certain degree of fertility. In the rich Fern Garden where everything grows mightily, I don't fertilize, and some daffodils and wood-hyacinths, as well as the volunteering dogtooth-violets, have prospered there for about a decade. In the small gardens and along the edge of the shrub borders, I fertilize heavily right after blooming while the embryo flowers for next spring are being formed inside the bulbs. Special fertilizers are available but superphosphate or bonemeal with unleached wood ashes is my favorite. I exercise great self-control and don't cut off the foliage until it is yellow, although I want to.

As I have suggested before, planting bulbs in groups with an open center space lets you introduce in-bud annuals, like tall impatiens in a shady place, a marigold or zinnia in the sun—to help cover the unsightly retreat. Or you can arrange your bulbs behind late-appearing perennials, astilbes or the balloon-flowers that will hide their maturing but not their previous flowering.

If you plant the small earlies where they will get winter sunlight and be warmed by nearness to a house wall, you'll have the thrill of late winter bloom. The golden green-collared aconites open under lilacs, close to the house and in view of the living room. Here, too, are snowdrops that are also "permanent" bulbs. To get a good show, plant a lot, at least fifty, of these little fellows, also the species crocus; a dozen or so doesn't add up to much, though in time they will seed and spread. I planted borders of the golden *Crocus chrysanthus* along the mailbox path, where I enjoy their March bravery because I have to walk that way at least once a day. And on the bank and under the rock there the 'King Alfred' daffodils open soon after. Keep in mind with daffodils that the flowers will turn toward the sun; this could prevent their facing where you want them to. The violet-blue chionodoxas appear late March to early April beneath the fringetree at the front steps, and in lucky years I've had the purple *Iris reticulata* in bloom at the kitchen windows. Of the cold-defying hyacinths I cannot have enough; I plant them beside the kitchen steps where their fragrance is enchanting. Elsewhere the pale yellow 'City of Harlaam' hyacinths make a lovely ribbon of contrast along the dark areas of pachysandra and ivy.

Below the south plant-room window under the Christmas-berry tree, the orange-red Greigii hybrid tulips come up year after year, so, too, later favorites under the apple tree and along the driveway. It's obvious I tuck bulbs in anywhere I can. Once set—and there's no argument about planting being a very big job—they stay with me for years.

Try to send in your bulb orders by early September; you will then get delivery of most before the end of the month. You *can* plant up till freezing weather but the bulbs like it better, and so will you, if you put them in through the golden weeks of late September and October.

Plant the big daffodil and tulip bulbs 6 to 8 inches apart and 8 to 10 inches deep, measured from the *bottom* of the hole. This is somewhat deeper than suppliers have the nerve to recommend but this way tulips don't run out or fail to show up the second year. Some of mine were set even lower, down 12 inches. The smaller species tulips need only 6-inch depths. The robust Dutch hyacinths, 8 inches apart, also need 8-to-10-inch depths or they will have to be staked, for with too shallow underground support, they topple over when heavy with rain.

Soak the aconite tubers twenty-four hours, then plant immediately, otherwise they may never show up. Cover them with 2 to 3 inches of soil, and keep watered through the first autumn; but I guarantee they will be on their own thereafter, seeding freely, with no further care from you.

Plant the other small bulbs—crocus, scillas, snowdrops, muscari—3 inches deep and 3 inches apart. Set them all firmly in each hole or in a large prepared area so that there are no air pockets underneath. When you have all the bulbs tucked away, give them a good watering.

See all these in one of the catalogues in color.

A crowd of golden daffodils lights up the slope beside the cliff. To get a natural effect when planting, throw the bulbs about from the bag and then plant them where they fall. Raymond photo.

Flowering Sequence of Spring Bulbs

Iris reticulata
Winter-aconite, *Eranthis hyemalis*
Crocus species
Snowdrops, *Galanthus*
Chionodoxa
Dutch Crocus
Dutch Hyacinths
Dogtooth-violet, *Erythronium*
Jonquil, *Narcissus jonquilla,* and miniature daffodils
Tulip species, *fosteriana, greigii, kaufmanniana*
Siberian Squill, *Scilla sibirica*
Grape-hyacinth, *Muscari*
Trumpet Daffodil
Single, Double Early, and Mendel Tulips
Large-cupped and Medium-cupped Daffodils
Daffodils, other types
Tulips, Triumph, Double Late, Lily-flowered, Parrot, and Darwin Hybrids
Tulips—Late Darwins, Cottage, and Breeder Varieties (long-stemmed)
Wood-hyacinths or Spanish Squills, *Scilla hispanica* (*campanulata*)

What Neat Edgings Can do. Good edgings do for your place what a fresh satin binding does for a shabby blanket or appropriate makeup for a plain woman. Keep the edgings neat and your garden is likely to look well groomed even if in back all is not perfection. Edgings of brick laid in sand look nice and avoid clipping. Also ridging edges with a "Dutch hoe" or other pointed tool that makes a channel deep enough to control grass spread into flower and shrub beds—easy work, too, no bending. I like my Reisch Handy Hoe that draws narrowly through the ground rather than chopping it in a wide furrow. (The address for it is Southington, Conn. 06489.)

These are my five favorite perennial edgers; I don't bother with annuals for edgings, though sweet-alyssum looks nice and smells good.

Candytuft, *Iberis.* White, spring-flowering evergreen for sun or shade. Plant the species *I. sempervirens* for a sprawling border to 15 inches wide, one of the smaller cultivars for a neat 12-inch edge. Shear back after bloom. To avoid winter burn and bloom loss on plants growing in southern or eastern exposures, apply an anti-desiccant spray like Wilt-Pruf, Formula NCF. Do this on an above-45-degree day in late November and again in February; definitely worth the bother. This candytuf edges my Look-Into Garden.

Coralbells, *Heuchera*. Red, white, pink, salmon, and a new chartreuse cultivar for sun or light shade, almost evergreen; the 10-by-15-inch plants with 18-inch clouds of bloom for six June-into-July weeks, lovely for bouquets. This edges my Apple-Tree Garden.

Jacobs-Ladder, *Polemonium reptans*. Lavender flowers and ferny foliage, a good fern companion, deciduous, for sun or light shade; 12-by-12-inch plants with spring blooms a little higher; cut back after bloom. Plant dies down for a month then renews, not for the prominence of iberis or heuchera but very lovely. This edges walks in the Round Garden.

Myrtle or Periwinkle, *Vinca minor*. Lavender or white late-spring flowers on an evergreen creeper. The 12-by-18-inch spreading plants thrive with some sun or in light or deep shade; they make a fine little hedge to clip occasionally if a straight edging is wanted. This edges my front doorstep garden and a number of broad shrub-and-evergreen plantings.

Pinks, Clove, *Dianthus plumarius*. Red, pink, or white spicy-fragrant flowers in May and intermittently till fall; on sprawling evergreen, glaucous, 6-by-18-inch mats, the blooms held a little above them. Full sun, lime-loving, only a few pinks are grown here because of the rather acid soil. Easy from seed.

Strawberry, *Fraises des Bois* types. White flowers, May on to frost with a wealth of summer-to-fall fruit. For these dependable, evergreen 8-by-12-inch plants, sun is essential. Charming and unusual, but I have too much shade here for them.

For the Pleasure of Fragrance. In the sixteenth century, Francis Bacon in his essay "Of Gardens" made the distinction between the flowers that are "free" of their fragrance and those that are "fast." "And because the breath of flowers is far sweeter in the air (where it comes and goes like the warbling of music) than in the hand, therefore nothing is more fit for that delight, than to know what be the flowers and plants that do best perfume the air." As we discover, the scent of most roses must be drawn in at close range while that of my rugosa beside the fence perfumes the air for yards around. Here is a list of plants to bring rich, far-reaching fragrance to your garden; almost all of these plants grow here.

PLANTS THAT DO BEST PERFUME THE AIR

PLANT	POPULAR NAME	TIME OF BLOOM
Buddleia alternifolia	garland butterfly-bush	Late May to early June
davidii	butterfly-bush	Late July to October
Chimonanthus praecox	wintersweet	January to mid-February
Chionanthus virginica	fringetree	Late May to mid-June
Clematis montana rubens	pink anemone clematis	Late May to June
paniculata	autumn clematis	August and September
Clethra alnifolia	sweet-pepperbush; summersweet	July and August
Crataegus oxyacantha	English May-tree	May
Dianthus plumarius and hybrids	cottage pinks	May and June
Hamamelis mollis	Chinese witch-hazel	February and March
Hyacinthus orientalis	common hyacinth	Mid-April to early May
Lilium auratum and hybrids	goldband lily	July and August
regale	regal lily; royal lily	July
Lonicera fragrantissima	winter honeysuckle	Late February to May
japonica halliana	Hall's honeysuckle	June to November
Magnolia stellata	Star magnolia	April
Malus baccata and hybrids	Siberian crab apple	Late April to mid-May
Muscari armeniacum	grape-hyacinth	Mid-April to early May
Narcissus jonquilla	jonquil	Mid-May
poetaz	poetaz narcissus	Late April to early May
Philadelphus coronarius and hybrids	mock-orange	Late May to mid-June
microphyllus and hybrids	mock-orange	Late May to mid-June
Phlox paniculata and forms	summer perennial phlox	Mid-July to late September
Populus candicans	balm-of-Gilead poplar	May
tacamahaca	balsam poplar	May
Prunus mume	Japanese apricot	March
Rhododendron aborescens	sweet azalea	June
roseum	rose-shell azalea	Mid-May
hybrids: Mollis, Ghent, Knaphill, Exbury, Ilam	azalea hybrids	Mid-May to mid-June
Ribes odoratum	clove-currant	Mid-April to mid-May
Rosa damascena bifera	Damask rose	Late May to mid-June and later
eglanteria (leaves only)	eglantine; sweetbrier	Mid-April on, in dampness
rugosa and forms		Late May to October
moschata hybrids	hybrid musk rose	Late May to October
Syringa vulgaris and forms	common lilac	Early May to June
Viburnum carlcephalum	fragrant snowball	Early May to late May
carlesii	pink snowball	Late April to May
Viola odorata	sweet violet	Late March to late April
Wisteria sinensis and hybrids	Chinese wisteria	Mid- to late May

Lighting the Garden

A night glow on choice plants or a favorite scene adds greatly to the pleasures of any garden. Here two lanterns on posts light the footbridge and the path above it. I often leave my reading chair in the living room to look out at the cheery scene. But the real joy comes from the broad beam that illuminates the brook and the dark rock beyond. We took a lot of trouble, my contractor Phil Punzelt and I, to select just the right location for this important garden light. Using a long extension cord, he moved the big temporary bulb about four times through one winter to various positions, first on one side of the brook, then on the other. Finally we found that casting the light *across* rather than into the brook was just right, so in the spring he ran a short underground cable from the house to a three-sided wooden box, this placed so as to be concealed by a stump over which I trained a mound of euonymus.

I cannot tell you the pleasure the night picture gives me, especially when the banks of the brook are covered with snow, the water trickling through icy margins, and the light dramatizing a scene dominated by the black cliff. On a snowy evening I can hardly move away from the west dining-room window that frames this exciting picture.

In recent years the possibilities of lighting gardens have been the concern of both electrical experts and landscape architects. Enchanting effects are possible with more sophisticated arrangements than mine, but even one well-placed light source that you work out for yourself can increase the pleasure of your garden for evening parties in summer as well as quiet times of meditation in winter.

Bird Books with Breakfast

Birds bring to the garden the excitement of motion and the gleam of color in the air. Attracting birds, watching their feeding, nest-building, and family life, even their antics—look at the nuthatch eating upside-down—are pleasures grown-ups and children can share. In this family we are always giving each other bird things for Christmas—nesting boxes, feeders, suet cakes, binoculars, and bird books. In fact, I serve guests bird books with breakfast since so many birds scratch and flutter about outside the kitchen casements. Next door the grandchildren, Susie and Eric, enjoy feeders hung outside their bedroom windows; from babyhood they have been bird-conscious.

This bird feeder, weatherproof and squirrel-proof and filled with a mixture of cracked corn, hemp, sunflower seeds, and millet, attracts a multitude, among them the cardinal, dove, junco, and song sparrow.

Below the study windows, I observe a feeder that is just about 100 percent squirrel-proof; only one agile creature got into it in nine years.

Obviously, there is nothing occult about attracting birds. The whole business just simmers down to food, water, and shelter. And a bird sanctuary can be started at any time of the year. It's in winter that our efforts seem particularly rewarding. As I write, there is a blizzard on and the whirling red wings of the cardinals and glinting white tail feathers of the juncos are beautifully exciting in the snow as the birds dash in and out of the feeder.

First consider food. Most birds are either seed-eating or insect-eating. Some are both but there is scarcely any bird that does not feed its nestlings insect food. Hence the value of birds to the gardener who needs plenty of help in getting rid of aphids and grubs. The basic feeding program includes a variety of grains for the seed-eaters; and for the insect-eaters, beef-kidney suet, especially in cold weather when bugs are scarce.

In our feeders a combination of sunflower seed, hemp, millet, and cracked corn of the baby-chick size (we get this mixture in twenty-pound bags) has proved a simple but attractive menu to the song sparrow, junco, cardinal, and dove. At first we scattered food on the ground since it is the nature of these birds to feed there. After some weeks, however, they discovered the above-ground storehouse, so we discontinued this wasteful method and let fall only a little through the sides of the feeder.

For the insect feeders we have a suet stick—a 2-foot section of 3-inch rough-barked tree limb. Scattered over this are about a dozen ¾-inch holes, ¾ inches deep bored slightly upward so that water will not lodge in them. These holes are filled with suet. This stick hangs on a fine wire from an ash tree and attracts the downy woodpeckers. Sometimes, too, the woodthrush lunges at it and eats without lighting, while the white-breasted nuthatch consumes quantities of suet in its own contrary position.

In another garden a coconut shell hangs from a magnolia tree and lures robins to a feast of seedless raisins; a shelf heaped with shelled peanuts attracts the bluebird, nuthatch, cardinal, chickadee, and song sparrow; apples cut in half draw the catbird, woodthrush, and robin.

Containers for bird food may be as simple as a shelf nailed to a stump in a sunny, out-of-the-wind spot or as fancy as a revolving glass hopper. There are many commercial feeders available with various devices to recommend each. A proper feeder "is a weather-proof storehouse for a quantity of food where the birds can get at it and other animals cannot." Blind alley feeders and small ones under a foot square are to be avoided, also metal ones since in freezing weather a bird may be blinded if its moist eye strikes some bit of icy metal.

Water for birds is just as pleasing to them in a large, flower pot saucer as in a handsome bath with sculptured adornment. The ideal birdbath, always filled with fresh, clean water, slopes gradually from the edge to a depth of not more than 2 inches in the center and with a rough surface to provide foothold.

A drying-room, that is a tree or shrub, should stand close-by so that birds with sodden plumage can safely dry, out of the reach of enemies from which they cannot readily fly. Thickets, which might conceal lurking cats, however, are to be avoided near birdbaths. Hollowed stones are appropriate to woodland sites; a pedestal birdbath shows to advantage the dazzling bluejays and delighted robins, as they bathe and drink. The only problem is keeping it filled in hot weather, when the splashing birds and evaporation empty it three times a day.

Food-bearing trees and shrubs also make a place attractive to birds. You may even take leave of neatness and let some area, the boundary line perhaps, go unpruned and uncultivated. Such an undisturbed thicket with a few evergreens offers both nesting sites and winter protection.

Research has been done on what berried plants attract what birds. In an old U.S. Farmers' Bulletin on "How to Attract Birds," I found such fascinating facts as this—106 birds go for the elderberry fruits, 86 for the dogwood, 73 for the bayberry, 52 the mulberry, and 45 the holly. The red-cedar, sassafras, mountain-ash, juneberry, snowberry, viburnum, honeysuckle, Virginia-creeper, and bittersweet are other favorites, as we notice here in fall when the birds begin stripping the juiciest highbush cranberry in September and the drier holly trees in the spring. From the Superintendent of Documents, Government Printing Office, Washington, D.C. 20402, you can now obtain two excellent leaflets, "Invite Birds to Your Home," with color illustrations (25¢) and "Homes for Birds," with helpful drawings showing how to make boxes (20¢).

Most suburban gardens have too few natural nesting sites. The song sparrows and field sparrows and the meadowlark, for example, want high grass or very low thickets. The cardinal likes a high thicket near human habitation and, once suited, stays for life, raising two or three broods a year and adorning a garden with permanent color and an enchanting whistle. We think the best luck any birder can have is to charm a cardinal. Our pair (one family tolerates no other within about an acre area) is the eternal delight of every member of the family and the brightest and most constant visitor to the feeder. The cardinal will never be lured into box nesting. The robin, however, will take to a tree or a three-sided house, or a 6-by-8-inch shelf; and 4-by-4-inch dwellings appeal to nuthatches, titmice, chickadees, and house wrens.

If there are no hollow trees or decaying limbs for the woodpeckers, flickers, crested flycatchers, and bluebirds, either commercial or home-made boxes may be supplied. Boxes should be roomy and well made, preferably of stoutly nailed 7/8-inch boards to keep out drafts, and with an overhanging roof which can be removed fall and spring so that old nests can be cleaned out. The entrance hole is made 2 inches from the top and just large enough for the wanted tenant to enter. Face boxes as nearly south as possible and place them either upright or slightly forward to keep out rain. Birds prefer plain, natural brown or green boxes and in rather sunny, open locations.

It is a good idea to put up wren and flicker boxes in the fall so they will have a winter's seasoning before the questing birds arrive. Clean out and spray old birdhouses with a contact insecticide early in February. You will not find really good birdhouses inexpensive, since strong, well-made ones with durable and removable roofs cannot be produced cheaply. Fine ones do last a long time, however, and are a good garden investment.

MY WHAT-TO-DO-WHEN LIST

A Month-by-Month Guide for the Dedicated

Here is the program that I follow pretty much from January through December. These are routine suggestions I hope you will find helpful in keeping your own planted place in hand. This isn't meant to be a goad list, although the energetic may find it so!

JANUARY

> Ring out the old, ring in the new;
> Ring, happy bells, across the snow;
> The year is going, let him go;
> Ring out the false, ring in the true.
>
> ALFRED TENNYSON

If ever there is a pause in the year's occupation it is this month, the turn of the year, when even the most ambitious gardener can take a few deep breaths without feeling guilty. Now is the time to dwell on the larger view, to dip into George Washington's *Diaries* of his Mount Vernon gardens, perhaps sample, as I like to, some of the old books by such grand gardeners as Gertrude Jekyll or Louise Beebe Wilder.

Snow Removal. Brush upwards, don't knock down heavy snow off bending birches and weighted evergreens, privet, other shrubs. Branches break off easily when snow forms an icy crust.

Wood Ashes. Store fireplace wood ashes *covered*—a wonderful source of potash for your lilacs, roses, and peonies.

Birds. Hang some feeders for bird-watching outside a bedroom window; nice to see cardinals up there on a snowy day.

View of the Month. A pair of intrepid mallards swimming against the current of the brook.

Diary Notes. January 31, 1959. Thermometer at zero this morning. Just a trickle through the center of the brook, but mallards busy there. My garden year started, planning Look-Into Garden outside the new kitchen. I want bloom there all the time.

FEBRUARY

> There are winter days so full of sudden sunlight that they will cheat the wise crocus into squandering its gold before its time.
>
> OSCAR WILDE

This is a forward-looking month when you need not press yourself unless you feel like it and have an urge to be outdoors on a pleasant day with its hint of spring.

Lawn Paths. Invite delivery boys and friends to keep to driveways and walks. Short cuts over snow-covered lawns now mean extra work in spring—and there will be plenty anyway. If there must be a path, lay boards to save the grass.

Pruning in General. On a decent sunny day when you won't hate the job, *start* pruning trees and any late-blooming shrubs, but know *why* you do it. To get rid of broken branches? To make plants more shapely? To admit light and air to areas beneath? To promote bloom by inducing new growth? Whatever your aim, *respect* the natural form; don't just saw off tops. (See Chapter 14.)

Pruning Clematis. As soon as leaf buds show this month or next on *C.* X *jackmanii,* 'Comtesse de Bouchard', 'Ernest Markham', 'Hagley Hybrid', 'Lady Betty Balfour', and 'Mme. Baron Veillard', cut plants back to 1 to 2 feet; thin out only weak and dead wood on 'Mme. Édouard André', 'Mrs. Cholmondeley', 'Henryi', 'Prins Hendrik', and 'Ramona' if you want big early flowers. (See Chapter 11.)

Seed Flats. Start collecting wooden or plastic seed flats and other containers to use next month for indoor sowing of the slower annuals.

Order Plants by the end of the month. How about trying something new, at least new to you, maybe a yellow-flowering *Laburnum* X *waterei (vossii)*, the goldenchain-tree, for late-May flowering or a *Magnolia stellata* for a fragrant April?

Assess Your Supplies. Fertilizers, mulching materials, dusts or sprays, and other needs, as stakes and plant ties. So comforting to have them on hand later, just when you need them.

Get Tools Sharpened. Pruners and mower can be attended to faster and cheaper now than by emergency later.

Perennials. Press back any heaved plants.

Birds. Watch now for the mourning doves—they love cracked chick corn—the wrens, the purple finches, and the bluebirds, so rare here lately. Woodpeckers will raid a suet feeder. Smearing pole or post with tanglefoot keeps off squirrels and even raccoons.

Diary Notes. February 4, 1963. A lot of excitement. This morning a doe came crashing down the east hill, ran across the brook, over the cliff, and across the road. Neighbors telephoned each other to look. Then a muskrat waddled up the snowy bank to the terrace, nibbled off a great branch of English ivy, more than half as big as he was, and waddled back to the stream. He swam like a streak with the ivy as sail below the bridge where he went under a tree with a nice green treat for the folks. Through the binoculars we saw cedar waxwings.

February 25, 1972. The first white blooms of the Christmas roses are opening in the Look-Into Garden, the plants knocked flat by the recent heavy snow. The aconites, tight little ovals, are bright yellow under the south living-room windows.

MARCH

> Ah, March! We know thou art
> Kindhearted, 'spite of ugly looks and threats,
> And out of sight are nursing April's violets.
>
> HELEN HUNT JACKSON

This is such a yes-and-no month with spring days to tempt you to uncover everything and winter days to wish you hadn't. It's a good idea to make haste slowly these end-of-winter weeks.

Lawns. Rake up the rough accumulation of winter when it's dry enough not to damage grass. On a windless day scratch, then seed bare spots; make a first application of fertilizer at mid-month when you see that grass is starting to grow; preferably use a high nitrogen, slow-release organic material, as a 10-6-4 or 15-8-12. A spreader makes the job easier, and coverage more even. If your grass is not even medium good but really terrible, perhaps you had better get a soil analysis and advice from your County Agricultural Agent. Send him soil samples scraped from the sides of trowel holes 6 inches deep and made at three different places on your lawn. Put them in separate polyethylene bags, marked for locality, as "front lawn," etc. If your lawn is small, mix the samples in one bag. No charge is made for this service in many states. (See Chapter 1 for my lawn procedures.)

Crabgrass Control. A vigorous stand of grass and good culture over several years usually win the battle. However, about once in three to five years, crabgrass may get out of hand. If last summer you saw great patches of it, better apply a pre-emergence chemical control (before grass shows up) early this month. This will seal the lawn surface, forming a barrier to sprouting crabgrass seed and, of course, other seed as well. Read the directions; some preparations allow sowing of grass seed ten days later.

Roses. Wait until the end of the month to uncover bushes; prune them at your convenience but before the leaf buds break. Don't try to prepare new beds until the ground is well thawed and the soil is workable. Clayey soils especially are damaged if spaded when wet; then later you have to break up the cemented clods. (See Chapter 9.)

Winter Losses. Don't be hasty in cutting back apparently dead wood on shrubs, but then don't wait forever for the gaunt specters to show signs of life. After one very cold winter, I cut back to the ground a sad mountain-laurel that by August put forth almost a foot of fresh new growth; also all of a 3-foot franklinia, except for one bit of green. By summer it had several new shoots and one 1-foot branch. I find plants do better when thus relieved fairly early of poor growth. The evergreen *Ilex crenata* almost always requires some cutting out of damaged wood but soon makes it up.

Pruning. On a pleasant "spring" day, while silhouettes are easy to assess, *continue* pruning trees and shrubs that have lost their figures; you sacrifice flowers on early bloomers but it's worth while to open up bad tangles as on old forsythias and weigelas; there's no flower sacrifice on peegee hydrangea, rose-of-Sharon, buddleia, and vitex that bloom late. (See Chapter 14.)

Seed Sowing Indoors. Sow seeds of tender or slow annuals that require eight weeks or more from planting to blooming in flats, pots, or coffee cans. Much more than an eight-week start indoors means too much transplanting or weak leggy plants. A not-too-hot sunny window sill (60 to 70° at night) is good or set seed pans under fluorescent lights. Try to limit yourself to a good crop of just one or two fine varieties of China aster, calendula, petunia, snapdragon (but allow these 10 to 12 weeks), stock, or verbena. Pelleted seeds are easier to handle. Or don't bother with any of this and buy from a florist or roadside stand in-bud plants when it's time to set them out in your garden. Good varieties are now offered this way or you can order them ahead from a local source.

Sowing Seed Outdoors. Sow *where they are to grow* seeds of bachelors-button, centaurea, chrysanthemum, larkspur (Giant Imperial is handsome), nicotiana, California and Shirley poppies, sweet-alyssum for edging, sweet peas (March 17 but only if your summers are not too hot; these are not easy), about a month before the last frost is likely in your area.

Clean Out Birdhouses but don't paint them.

Diary Notes. March 28, 1964. Just warm enough for weeding though below freezing every morning so the yellow crocuses along the mailbox path hardly show. Birds everywhere, flickers, a bluebird next door, and a purple finch; pheasants wandering around again on the bare hill.

March 26, 1967. Two blizzards this month, almost a foot of snow with Christmas roses in full bloom; hyacinths pointing up since mid-January, daffodils show 3 inches.

March 1, 1972. Record heat, 73 degrees; I fear for the plants encouraged to grow when doubtless there is freezing, or worse, weather to come. Only the flowers in the bulbs won't mind; they seem conditioned to extremes.

APRIL

> For, lo, the winter is past, the rain is over and gone; the flowers appear on the earth; the time of the singing of birds is come, and the voice of the turtle is heard in our land.
>
> THE SONG OF SOLOMON

This month and the next are times when your planted place seems to require you to move in ten directions at once. Don't do it. Spring is too lovely not to keep a few hours for savoring. Consider what is said below as guide not drive. Some chores can just as well be done later.

Lawns. If you haven't renovated yet, better get at it first thing. Don't go in for a big dig-up. There's always something to save. (See March advice; also Chapter 1.)

Apply First All-Purpose Spray for pest-and-disease control on ornamentals, April 15 to May 1. (See Chapter 15.)

Roses. Work fertilizer lightly into soil when it is thawed enough, water it in well in dry weather. Cut back farther if dead stubs show above your previous cuts. As leaves develop, apply first weekly all-purpose spray or dust. For constant dooryard bloom, plant 'The Fairy', pink, low, and shrubby; for superb fragrance, the tall damask shrub roses 'Kazanlik' and 'Celsiana'. (See Chapter 9.)

Prune Hollies lightly to shapeliness; rake up their leaves shed *naturally;* apply acid fertilizer, say 5 pounds under leaf-spread of a 6-foot tree; water deeply; spread a coarse pine-bark or wood-chip mulch.

Perennials. Clean up beds and fertilize over the old mulch. Add 3 pounds of ammonium sulphate to an equal amount of a 5-10-5 fertilizer to compensate for the nitrogen taken from soil by bacteria as they decompose the mulch. Late in the month, or early in May, divide late-summer and fall-blooming types—phlox, asters, and chrysanthemums—and reset the young outside growth, discarding the hard centers. For more summer and autumn color, plant purple platycodons and golden heleniums—both very hardy.

Peonies. Set supports in place as shoots emerge. Use a readymade tripod ring or a wide cylinder of 2-inch wire mesh 18 inches high for each plant.

To Avoid Borer on German Iris. Clean out old leaves and debris and spray with malathion when leaves are 6 inches tall. Specialists advise repeating at 10-day intervals until flower spikes appear.

Herbs. Set out a little perennial herb patch in the sun, preferably near the kitchen door—chives, orégano, sage, thyme—with a sowing of parsley for edging. Give the useful but invasive mints a place of their own.

Diary Notes. April 29, 1964. I've done a tremendous amount of man's work on the brook hill where I moved two great accumulations of leaves that were smothering the new laurels and daffodils; marsh-marigolds out and there's a good spread of them. Virginia bluebells planted last year coming up. Set out a group of white pines to cut the view of another new house; also, some hemlocks to conceal the neighbor's trash.

MAY

> It is a golden maxim to cultivate the garden for the nose, and the eyes will take care of themselves.
>
> ROBERT LOUIS STEVENSON

Plant for fragrance; this is a highly scented month here, "like a Paris boutique," one visitor said. It's the species azaleas, the aromatic leaf buds unfolding on the balm-tree and the lilacs that perfume the air.

Weed, Fertilize, and Mulch. Get out every weed from the flower beds; apply a plant food high in phosphorus, a 4-12-4 perhaps (which I follow in fall with an organic, such as bonemeal). Then spread a 2-to-3-inch mulch. Mulches are your greatest ally for conserving moisture, inhibiting weeds. Avoid peatmoss or buckwheat hulls, which incline to blow away; instead, use redwood bark or pine bark or wood chips.

Apply Second All-purpose Spray for pest- and disease-control about May 15. (See Chapter 15.) Or try a systemic pest control. I have been using systemic preparations with success. On 'New Dawn' and other vigorous roses, no other protection has been needed. Systemics have also controlled leafminer on birches, hollies, and photinia, and I am hoping they will keep the laburnum free of black aphids. Of course, systemics are poisonous but there is little danger if they are worked *into* the soil under trees and bushes and then watered in well. (See Chapter 15.)

More Pruning. If you have let shrubs get out of hand, do a big pruning job now on the early spring bloomers, especially shadbush and overgrown forsythias. (See Chapter 14.) If attended to yearly, this is a simple task, but the removal of old woody growth from the center of neglected plants is not child's play! However, even hard work in the garden is pleasant on a balmy day in May.

Roses. Cut out suckers (canes with seven instead of five leaflets) close to main stem below the soil line; train new growth on climbing roses; continue weekly dusting or spraying.

Hardy Bulbs. Fertilize while hyacinths, narcissus, tulips, etc. are still in growth and making embryo flowers for next year. (I use superphosphate along with unleached wood ashes.) Don't remove foliage until it dies down naturally, but you can cut flower stems to ground for neatness.

Groundcovers. Clean up, water deeply as necessary, weed, and fertilize pachysandra, ivy, and myrtle; once weed-choked, groundcovers are difficult to get right again. Trim back ivy and myrtle and thin out plants if you need them to extend your plantings elsewhere.

Christmas and Lenten Roses. Fertilize and mulch these hellebores now but don't move old plants unless absolutely necessary; like peonies they prefer a settled life.

Seeds to Sow. When soil has warmed up (but don't be in too big a hurry; frost sometimes occurs here as late as May 14), sow the tender annuals—balsam, marigold, nasturtium, salvia, zinnia, also some of the attractive dwarf hybrid dahlias.

Impatiens. Order plants of this sure-fire bloomer (for *shade*) early so as to get it in the more effective separate colors. The white is lovely in a north location as an interplanting with maturing hyacinths. It blends nicely with pachysandra, is a pleasant base for an espaliered pyracantha.

Lawns. There is only the eternal mowing now—for most grasses not lower than 1½ to 2 inches on established lawns but 2 inches for sure on new grass. I am not in favor of rolling, which only seems to speed compaction. Let short clippings remain to mulch the grass plants but use a catcher for long clippings or rake up a big accumulation to avoid fungus troubles. A compost pile reserved exclusively for grass soon decays.

Watering. If May is dry, start a schedule of thorough deep watering. Trees and shrubs planted within the last two years, peonies and roses forming buds and flowers—all need plenty of moisture. Never let a new lawn area get dry or grass seeds won't germinate. For that matter, it is calculated that even an established lawn needs an inch of water a week to keep it green when the temperature stays above 70 degrees.

Lawn Weeds. If you don't do anything else, pick the dandelion flowers; your problem will really be compounded if you let plants go to seed. Dig out the broadleafs, my way with an asparagus knife; it's a rewarding task on a nice day for you can always see where you've worked. But if the job looks momentous, apply a lawn weed-killer with your spreader. For best results, wait for a warm day, at least 70 degrees. *Warning:* If you have, and want to keep clover, as I do, read the weed-killer label to see if it is also a clover-killer.

Diary Notes. May 20, 1957. "Magic lantern flowers" on wisteria exquisite; new arbor due to go up June 3, should make even this ambitious vine happy. Everything smells divine; the fringetree is coming out and all the lilacs. A phoebe made a nest at the front door while I was away and has hatched five of the smallest items I've ever seen. Now we do not use the front door, and have turned on no lights for a month. What to do tomorrow night for the birthday party? A nesting bird quite a limiting factor.

May 9, 1959. A wonderful world of flowers, fragrance, and birds—doves, redwing blackbirds, robins nesting in the ilex, bluejays and cardinals on the feeder morning and evening; brownthrasher, flickers, song sparrows. They wheel up in my view as I sit at the desk—terribly distracting. Apple-Tree Garden in full splendor.

May 13, 1960. Spring so late forsythia and pink crab apples blooming together.

May 15, 1963. Poor spring; cold with driving winds, just when trees and bulbs are at height. Yellow and pink-green 'Fantasy' tulips lovely together. Purple tulips and purple hyacinths even with the white house as background need yellow and white with them. I think the skunk cabbage and false hellebores in the Fern Garden are two of the handsomest plants possible, and the lanceleaf iris makes a fine contrast.

May 5, 1965. Leaf raking goes on; more leaves than trees here. Three kinds of violets—white, speckled lavender, and Confederate; yellow doronicum, Virginia bluebells, and pink bleedinghearts, a lovely combination.

JUNE

> My garden, with its silence and the pulses of fragrance that come and go on the airy undulations, affects me like sweet music. Care stops at the gates, and gazes at me wistfully through the bars. Among my flowers and trees, Nature takes me into her own hands, and I breathe as freely as the first man.
>
> ALEXANDER SMITH

This is the last colorful "spring" month here. After this, there will still be small areas of bloom but mostly the emphasis will be on cool green in the shade of trees.

Pruning Early Shrubs. On deutzia, mock-orange, shadbush, spirea (not 'Anthony Waterer' yet), and weigela, cut out about one-third of any tough old growth right at the ground line; also remove some of the crowding new growth. Shape to promote open development and a pleasing *natural* outline. You can also cut back side branches one third. (See Chapter 14.)

Prune Lilac, Rhododendron, Mountain-Laurel. To improve their looks, remove faded flower clusters if you can manage this big job. Take care not to damage the two buds just below this year's flower truss on lilacs for they are next year's flowers. Don't worry if it's all too much trouble. These shrubs will bloom next year despite seed heads, the new growth pushing beyond them.

Apply Third Spray for pest-and-disease control about June 1. (See Chapter 15.)

Watering. Drought sometimes occurs this month just when the steady growth of everything requires moisture. Always water deeply, with sprinklers usually left not less than an hour in each place, the slow-running hose 30 minutes beside small newly planted shrubs, an hour beside big ones, longer for evergreens. You can measure the amount of water applied by a sprinkler by setting a coffee can at the outer edge of the spray. Move the sprinkler when an inch accumulates.

Astilbes. Discover these perfect perennials with ferny foliage and spires of fragrant bloom. Rarely bothered by pests, they are easy to grow in light shade with some moisture, fine to cut. Good varieties: 'White Deutschland', Pink 'Peach Blossom', garnet 'Fanal', salmon 'Granat'. Good companions for pale varieties in my garden are ferns, Lenten-roses, and Japanese iris.

Japanese Iris. Plant *Iris kaempferi* with its 6-to-10-inch blooms that open after the first delphiniums and before summer phlox to fill in sometimes dull weeks in the garden. Colors, beside white, are deep and jewel-like purple, rose, and blue. My favorites: 'Queen of the Blues' and the white 'Gold Bound'. Provide a well-drained site, soil rich in organic matter and abundant moisture, especially during the growing season. The swordlike foliage makes a fine foil for fluffy bunch growers. The yellow lupinelike thermopsis and the yellow meadowrue, *Thalictrum glaucum,* are also good companions. This iris is lovely beside pools.

Hyacinths and Early Narcissus. Cut off yellowing tops but wait a bit longer for late-flowering narcissus and tulips.

For Neatness. Trim back myrtle that is out of bounds along garden walks. Shear tops of evergreen candytuft, *Iberis,* to thicken growth for next spring's snowdrift of bloom.

Roses. Unless you have successfully applied a pesticide-fungicide systemic, dust or spray roses regularly—usually every seven to ten days from now until October to keep plants in health and looks. Wastefully, I have used an all-purpose dust for everything untoward, not quite proper, but it saves thinking about which to apply for what. Remove faded blooms, and on new bushes cut the fresh blooms with *short* stems. Disbud Hybrid Teas only if you want large blooms or plan to exhibit.

Peonies. Transplant nonblooming peonies if they are crowded or in deep shade; let blooming plants alone for years and years. When you get to it, apply a generous handful of superphosphate around each plant.

Diary Notes. June 6, 1957. Rainbow for breakfast on the terrace;

the ring sprinkler on the lawn caught a perfect arc while we ate hot cakes.

June 6, 1962. Drought, brook only a trickle; feeling sad, many dead elms removed, but discovered a big Norway maple back of Round Garden; this can be pruned to a handsome silhouette as backdrop to replace elms there; left one elm stump for a birdpath pedestal.

June 15, 1963. Hardly a month of moonlight and roses; weeds in awesome abundance; also inchworms. The thousand daffodils that delighted me in April and May are now 10,000 leaves that must be allowed to mature to the flopping point but in all things, a breaking point, mine definitely this date. I cut and cut to make the Fern Garden neat again. Still fighting woodchucks, also rabbits. Daylilies chewed; which one did it?

June 15, 1971. Marvelous color achieved: purple and white clematis, pink-to-white laurel, coralbells, purple and white brook iris, 'Coral Magic' petunias, same color impatiens, lavender petunias, blue browallia, yellow hemerocallis. White tradescantia by the brook looks exactly right. Lilies under the fringetree coming into bloom in the shade in their eighth year.

JULY

> Summer afternoon—summer afternoon; to me those have always been the two most beautiful words in the English language.
>
> HENRY JAMES

Let up now. If summer sets in "with its usual severity" and the heat and humidity are unbearable, don't force yourself—or your husband—to do much in the garden. (My plant diaries moan over July heat, drought, and humidity.) Just sit outdoors and fan or inside with the air conditioner. Remember your planted place is for your pleasure, not, as I have said, an exercise in character development. Most big jobs can wait.

To Break the Drought. Simply plan an outdoor wedding or garden party with more guests than you can possibly accommodate indoors and the locked heavens will open. For three years this procedure has proved infallible for me.

Midsummer Controls. By this time, garden beds are likely to be choked with lush growth. Cut back the sprawling annuals to prevent their blooming out, setting seed, and interfering with your less rampant spring-flowering perennials. Cut back and thin out, too, the more violent perennials, as physostegia overrunning everything in reach, cinnamon ferns crowding into new clumps of daylilies. In the wild garden, pull out *all* the rampant meadow buttercups and you will have just the amount you want next spring. Cut back the spiderwort, *Tradescantia,* to ensure good September bloom.

Spray with an all-purpose fungicide to control disease if the thermometer and the hygrometer together indicate degrees adding up to 150. There's sure to be trouble when it's that hot and humid. (See Chapter 15.)

Violas. Cut back sharply; water deeply and mulch. Maybe they will prove perennial for you.

Climbing Roses. Prune some cool evening just after the spring ones stop blooming. Proceed according to type. (See Chapter 9.)

Hedges. With sharp shears, prune wider at base than top so that moisture and light can reach the whole plant.

Chrysanthemums. Pinch back tips for last time.

Train Vines Where You Want Them. This means almost weekly tying. Nothing is prettier than well-guided growth on clematis, fleece-vine, and wisteria; nothing is more graceless than great messy tangles. For tidiness and good wisteria bloom, let new plants develop only one or two leaders.

Separate German Iris now and up to September if flowers are getting smaller and stems shorter. Every three or four years is usually often enough. Divide each clump into two or three sections (but not single pieces). Trim fan tops back halfway. Reset the small outside divisions 12 inches apart, discarding the thick centers.

Diary Notes. July 3, 1963. Getting crabgrass under control with earlier pre-emergence treatment. Scillas good investment; in two years each bulb made about thirty. New Cascade Petunias from Geo. J. Ball, Inc., white, purple, pink, handsome; potted them for front steps with yellow lantana and purple heliotrope. Set out a dwarf pine at kitchen corner; hope it stays small.

July 1964. Dreadful month: drought, slugs, fungus, red spider; only the daylilies are inspiring.

AUGUST

When the glass is at ninety a man is a fool
Who directs not his efforts to try to keep cool.

JOSEPH ASHBY-STERRY

So direct yours that way. If you have put your faith and early efforts in mulching, you too can keep cool.

Lawns. Mow by the weather, not by the calendar. Through very dry weeks, you had better skip mowing, unless you have watered enough to keep the grass green and growing.

Watering. If rainfall is slight, let the slow-running hose gently soak newly planted trees and shrubs and also established plantings of rhododendrons, mountain-laurel, ferns, and perennials until moisture seeps well down. I allow about two hours for each area, and do I keep busy! Because of fungus troubles in this shady place, I stop watering before dark, then, as I have said, I put the hoses in position for next morning so I can turn the faucets on at the house without getting my feet soaked by dew.

Roses. Fertilize with fall bloom in view, and water plants deeply in dry spell.

Evergreens. Prune for shapeliness; transplant as new growth indicates root activity or wait till next month.

Lilies-of-the-Valley. Divide when blooms get sparse and small and the planting is mostly leaves. I dig up whole clumps and set them elsewhere. In a variety of locations, you can enjoy a longer period of bloom. I fill in the holes in the old plantings with well-enriched compost and sprinkle a little over the whole area to give them new life. Too little light and starvation are the usual cause of decline. Some sunlight is essential.

Bulbs. Order your bulbs of madonna lilies; they need to go in as soon as possible while the weather favors rooting.

Daylilies. After a rain is a good time to divide and transplant big clumps.

Take a Vacation!

Diary Notes. August 14, 1957. Put up wire basket of suet in lilac beside porch; brown thrashers, mother and child, love it; child as big as mother but insists with open beak that mother feed it; chica-dees constant, also catbirds. New standing bird feeder apparently squirrel-proof; sunflower seed brings cardinal and doves. Summer-sweet and tiger lilies lovely in an old brown earthenware pitcher on the porch.

August 15, 1963. Cool month, 52 degrees this morning, good rains. Endless lawn work—weed-killer again; brown spots look like fungus trouble, not coming back with rain. I'm sick of this lawn! Staked and tied, then moved larger royal ferns; sprayed tops and watered well; didn't miss a beat; I find I can transplant when I wish; the key is, water top and bottom.

August 1964. Golden trumpet-vine (not the orange one) nice with second blooming of purple 'Ramona' clematis and white 'Henryi'. Watering eternal. Tuberous begonias unhappy in heat and humidity; all-purpose dusting checks fungus, looks awful, will syringe off as soon as days are cooler.

SEPTEMBER

> Safe in the earth they lie, serenely waiting;
> They never speak to north winds or to snow,
> Perfume and color in the dark creating,
> Fit for the sunlit world that they will know.
>
> "Bulbs," LOUISE DRISCOLL

This really is a hard-working month when the weather usually co-operates with the changes you have been considering through summer. It's a pleasant time for transplanting, much better than hectic spring weeks when cold and rain often make outdoor work hard to plan and also unpleasant.

Lawns. Make a mighty effort! Your work counts most this month. This is the time for heavy all-over seeding, not spring when you should only spot-sow. The weather now is ideal for your purpose, with fall rains, longer nights, and cooler days. (See Chapter 1 on seed mixtures, etc.)

Wisteria. Early in the month, give vines a *light* last pruning, cutting back every new growth about halfway unless it is so rampant you must do more. (Too late pruning sacrifices bloom.)

Bulbs. Get your order in early this month. On your order sheet put data as to height, color, and location for planting and keep a copy for reference. Otherwise between ordering (when enthusiasm is high) and planting (when it recedes), you may forget, as I do, what goes where, and find yourself standing in the cold with a handful of tulip bulbs and not the foggiest idea what to do with them.

Daffodils. Open bags on arrival and keep in a cool place until you are ready to plant. Early planting allows deep rooting. Prepare soil well with compost or peatmoss and bonemeal. Daffodils will thrive a long while in the same place if the soil is good and bulbs have room to multiply. (Some of mine have been in handsome residence for ten years.) In beds, space big types 12 inches apart; cover *tips* with 5 inches of soil. If you want to plant a "drift," stand in one place, throw the bulbs around you, and plant where each falls; this way you'll get a natural effect.

Peonies. You could move them now if they aren't blooming well in spring, but maybe you should first try overhead pruning of trees or shrubs in case shade is the cause of trouble. Too deep planting, buds blasted by botrytis blight, or too little fertilizer for these big consumers are other possibilities to check before you decide to transplant.

Diary Notes. September 12, 1963. In England and Germany: Strong fragrance of lemon from espaliered magnolias at Goodwood in Sussex; scent of masses of white nicotiana in Cheyney Walk in London; at Planten un Blomen in Hamburg overpowering musky scent of sweet alyssum; climate cooperates in both countries and mass plantings do the rest.

September 18, 1963. Returned to find place had missed me; no watering through drought; lawn browned, calling county agent for advice.

OCTOBER

> But who can paint
> Like Nature? Can Imagination boast,
> Amid its gay creation, hues like hers?
>
> JAMES THOMSON

Such a colorful month is this my favorite. The white birches are dropping their golden triangles; the tulip-tree and beech are a beautiful yellow; the sugar maple is richly hued. Dogwoods, sumac, and some oaks are red, and the deciduous ferns everywhere are going into their russet hues. The larch is becoming a golden torch.

Leaves and Compost. Sweep leaves from grass to avoid soggy matting. Other places you can let them collect for that final-final haul out. Many trees do not make light work, but think now of compost with all this lovely leafy nitrogen ready to decay. A simple, out-of-sight leaf pile will do with a depression in the center to catch the rain. For a big place with many leaves, make a rough bin with old boards marking out a 12-by-12-foot space, the boards as high as your supply permits. If you have a lot of oak leaves, you could pile these separately; oak decays more slowly than other leaves and has a special value for acid plants.

Shrubs. Set these out, as many as you have room for as soon as they have lost their leaves. Deciduous shrubs with bulbs are the best possible low-upkeep plants with every landscape advantage of flowers and fruit as well. Perhaps let *Cornus mas* and *Lonicera fragrantissima,* the winter honeysuckle, start your spring procession as they do mine, and let the season close with the *Franklinia.*

Watering. Mid-month give all new plantings a thorough soaking, established ones also if there has been little rain; otherwise winter losses can be considerable.

Birds. Include food plants for birds. Where cats abound and neighbors don't bell them, you can rely on food plants instead of feeders. Here, these plants attract a multitude of birds: bayberry, dogwood, elder, hawthorn, honeysuckle, Japanese barberry, fruiting junipers, mulberry, shadbush, small-fruited crab apples, viburnums; also hemlock and white birch. Assure an unfrozen water supply—a big flower-pot saucer with a short log in it seldom freezes over.

Chrysanthemums. Early this month you might like to enjoy these flowers the way I do. Buy well-budded plants in pots. Group them near the house, along the front steps, and place them on *top* of the garden beds rather than in them. After plants stop blooming, I give them away to someone with plenty of garden space for them. In-bud plants are a nice extravagance and even a few go a long colorful way.

Bulbs. Plant as many daffodil, tulip, hyacinth, and crocus as you can; there's no such thing as enough of these in spring.

Autumn Leaf Fall. Note the time of leaf fall; convenient if all the leaves came down at once; here by mid-month the white birch, ash, and balm trees are bare; willow, tulip-tree, cherry, Norway maple, hawthorn, and crab apple are still green; apple and sweetgum, also the littleleaf linden and American plane-tree often hold their leaves bothersomely far into November. Latest of all is the giant wisteria and 'Ramona' clematis. I think their leaves will never fall and let me get the place cleaned up for winter.

Diary Notes. October 10, 1962. Back hill ablaze with sugar maples, sumac, woodbine that has climbed up in elms (both dead and alive ones) and one brilliant red oak. Spectacular fruiting on crab apples; big one beside drive needs heavy pruning; pair at lawn edge shapely, well suited to site. Planted hemlocks on west hill to block out firehouse, comforting to have near but not pretty. Laid out Round Garden, planted laurel circle. Sifted decayed compost on poor lawn areas. Inserted split flower pots around clematis to protect brittle stems.

October 22, 1963. Planted royal azalea in birch-tree bed. At A.H.S. Convention heard about systemics for leafminer; Connecticut Extension says too poisonous but I mean to try it; advised Sevin to control fruit development on apple tree but this produced the biggest crop of rotten fruit I've ever had to gather.

NOVEMBER

> November is a halfway month, halfway between fall and winter; halfway between the reds and gold of October and the grays of December . . . It is the month of browns.
>
> HAYDN S. PEARSON

My wish this month: I'd like never to see another leaf not firmly glued to a tree. Also, I wish I'd never heard that so-true old adage: *Leave the garden in the fall the way you want to find it in the spring.* I know that every weed pulled now, every grass seed sown, every clean-up operation mercifully counts against the spring turmoil, but at the season's end I long now for peace, not work, on my planted place.

Tulips. It's not quite too late to set out bulbs; water them well to hasten root development before soil freezes hard.

Lilies. Prepare the soil for these and mark the locations early in the month; then planting later when bulbs finally arrive won't be such a bone-chilling job. (See Chapter 10.)

Outdoor Faucets and Gutters. Drain faucets and clean out leaves from gutters if these are open. Strips of heavy wire mesh fastened over gutters here now avoid the tiresome ladder job. Rain gets through but not leaves and down spouts don't stop up.

Arbor Painting. Vines can be safely taken down now. I drape the big 'Ramona' clematis over a high stepladder, and then carefully tie it in place again when the paint dries.

Gravel Drives. Rake smooth to avoid frozen ruts later. Place markers while you can still pound them into the ground. I use heavy iron stakes with red glass eyes. They make good guide lines for snow removal and keep *most* inept drivers from circling out over the lawn.

Winter Protection. Spray Wilt-Pruf or a similar anti-desiccant on newly planted material and on any evergreens not reliably hardy or subject to sunburn in winter. I apply it only to the hardy candytuft edging of the Look-Into Garden. Otherwise winter sun on this small evergreen burns the flower buds. Anti-desiccants can often take the place of teepees on your evergreens for they prevent wind as well as sun damage. And do water well if autumn weeks are dry.

Roses in subzero land. If these are your joy, you have work ahead once the soil is on its way to deep freeze. To avoid wind damage, cut canes of Hybrid Teas, Floribundas, and Grandifloras back to 20 to 30 inches. To protect from severe cold, as well as alternate freezing and thawing, mound soil up around plants 10 to 12 inches. Do this after a 2-to-3-inch hard frozen crust has formed. Don't pull soil out of the beds but bring it in from another location. Then give additional protection of evergreen boughs, salt hay, coarse straw, or oak leaves; other leaves get soggy. This extra covering insulates soil mounds and prevents washing. Species and shrub roses need no protection and along Long Island Sound it is rarely necessary for the others. We do not cover plants here. If, where you live, cold is severe, rose bushes must be heavily wrapped, or covered with paper tubing, or protected by wooden structures.

Diary Notes. November 15, 1962. Picked last white pansies, plants still green, perhaps they will winter over; putting up two slatted compost bins in convenient areas; will save long hauls.

November 12, 1963. Fairly warm, heavy rains, another big elm and six small ones removed; replaced with a tulip-tree and a sophora beside brook; extending groundcovers; dote on pachysandra.

November 22, 1964. Mowed lawn again, will this grass never stop growing; some yellow primrose still blooming; watered new pines and laurel deeply; Wilt-Pruf on hardy candytuft; planted tubs at front door with small upright yews.

November 1965. Replaced tubbed yews with green pyramids of English ivy, must remember to water.

DECEMBER

> At Christmas I no more desire a rose
> Than wish a snow in May's new-fangled mirth;
> But like of each thing that in season grows.
>
> WILLIAM SHAKESPEARE

Reflection on the End of the Year. This is a time to be complacent. With all possible outdoor tasks completed—or forget them if they aren't—let's enjoy the winter views from our windows, the silhouettes of trees, the dark hues of evergreens, the nice property design we've worked out. Let's also enjoy fireside hours and read in safety about the dangerous exploits of plant hunters or study the advice of landscape designers. Maybe this winter we can come upon ideas to make our planted places still less work and even more in tune with the pleasure principle.

Christmas Tree. Select a live specimen early. While the ground is still open, dig a big, ample hole, then put the soil back. To prevent freezing, mulch the area with 10 inches of leaves held in place with boards. Indoors, keep your tree well watered and as cool as possible, turning off nearby radiators. Set your tree out as soon after Christmas as you can bear to part with it. Plant at the same level it grew before and firm soil around it. Replace mulch and hold it down with pine boughs. Spray with an anti-desiccant to reduce moisture loss.

Holly. Prune older trees freely for decoration; drastic side pruning results in thicker central growth later.

Cold Protection. After the first hard freeze—not simply a touch of frost—mulch perennials that require it to keep them cold and unstimulated by occasional midwinter warmth. Pull the mulching under, not over, green-topped plants. After their first year, leave uncovered peonies, iris, Oriental poppies, and delphinium (except in very cold sections). Daylilies never need a cover.

Tools. Clean and store lawn mower under a plastic cover. Clean and oil your usable tools; throw out the bent and rusted impossibles. Put tools on your Christmas list. My Wilkinson pruners are a joy—small for flowers, medium-sized for general use (kept in a jewelry box to avoid abuse by helpers), and a two-handled lopper.

Icy Drives and Sidewalks. To avoid grass and shrub damage, spread sand, Kitty Litter, fertilizer, or wood ashes, not rock salt that damages plants as it melts.

Noel for Lawn Weeds. Never give up. On mild days before freezing, take your winter exercise with an asparagus knife, digging out weeds that have resisted weed-killers but won't resist the long thrust and sharp turn of this excellent tool and your purposeful attention. If Christmas Day itself is rather warm for the season, lawn weeding is fine escape work and also helps to equalize the dinner of the year.

Diary Notes. December 15, 1965. Peace at last; looking not working, only thinking how to improve winter pictures; east hill handsome now that leaves have fallen and trees are in silhouette. West hill beautiful too—water, rock, snow. No question, I love this place, I'll keep it!

No matter how cleaned up I am when they come in, my friends say they always see one to three pairs of *wet* shoes at the back door, evidence of my only just-stopped activity in the garden; one visitor, Walter Haring, took this picture on arrival on a one-pair day.

Where to Buy

First see what your local nursery or garden center offers, particularly when the color of a plant is important. Then consider this brief selection of reliable firms with helpful catalogues.

J. Herbert Alexander, Middleboro, Massachusetts 02346 . . . lilacs, blueberries, Japanese quinces; perennials, groundcovers, vines.

Alpenglow Gardens, 13328 King George Highway, North Surrey, B.C., Canada . . . ferns, wildflowers, dwarf conifers. 25¢

Armstrong Nurseries, Box 473, Ontario, California 91764 . . . roses. Catalogue in color, $1.

Blackthorne Gardens, 48 Quincy Street, Holbrook, Massachusetts 02343 . . . lilacs.

Brimfield Gardens Nursery, 245 Brimfield Road, Wethersfield, Connecticut 06109 . . . trees and shrubs, many rarities; groundcovers, ferns, bamboo. 25¢.

W. Atlee Burpee Co., Philadelphia, Pennsylvania 19132 . . . general, flower seeds, some nursery stock.

Cadwell & Jones, Inc., 355 Park Avenue, East Haven, Connecticut 06108 . . . fertilizers and supplies.

Country Garden Roses, 555 Irwin Lane, Santa Rosa, California 95401 . . . roses.

P. deJager & Sons, South Hamilton, Massachusetts 01982 . . . bulbs.

Dutch Mountain Nursery, Route 1, Box 67, Augusta, Michigan 49012 . . . trees and shrubs; plants for birds and conservation.

Gardens of the Blue Ridge, Ashford, McDowell County, North Carolina 28603 . . . hardy ferns and wildflowers.

D. S. George Nurseries, 2491 Penfield Road, Fairport, New York 14450 . . . clematis.

Girard Nurseries, Geneva, Ohio 44041 . . . trees and shrubs; azaleas and rhododendrons.

Jackson & Perkins, Medford, Oregon 97501 . . . roses. Catalogue in color.

Joseph J. Kern Rose Nursery, Box 33, Mentor, Ohio 44060 . . . old roses.

Lamb Nurseries, E. 101 Sharp Avenue, Spokane, Washington 99202 . . . ferns and wildflowers; shrubs, vines, groundcovers, herbs.

Leslie's Wild Flower Nursery, 30 Summer Street, Methuen, Massachusetts 01844 . . . ferns and wildflowers; plants and seed. 25¢.

Walter Marx Gardens, Boring, Oregon 97009 . . . perennials. 50¢.

Mayfair Nurseries, R.D. 2, Nichols, New York 13812 . . . trees and shrubs; dwarf conifers and dwarf shrubs; groundcovers. 25¢.

Charles H. Mueller, River Road, New Hope, Pennsylvania 18938 . . . bulbs.

Geo. W. Park Seed Co., Greenwood, South Carolina 29646 . . . flower seeds, some rarities; summer bulbs, ornamental grasses.

Putney Nursery, Putney, Vermont 05346 . . . wildflowers and ferns; herbs, some general nursery stock; 25¢.

Rainier Mt. Alpine Gardens, 2007 South 126 Street, Seattle, Washington 98168 . . . rhododendrons, azaleas, dwarf evergreens.

Schreiner's, Route 2, Salem, Ohio 97303 . . . iris. 50¢.

Louis Smirnow, 85 Linden Lane, Glen Head P.O., Brookville, Long Island, New York 11545 . . . tree peonies. Catalogue in color.

Joel W. Spingarn, 1535 Forest Avenue, Baldwin, New York 11510 . . . trees and shrubs, dwarf conifers.

Star Roses, The Conard-Pyle Co., West Grove, Pennsylvania 19390 . . . roses, some perennials, shrubs. Catalogue in color.

Tillotson's Roses, 802 Brown's Valley Road, Watsonville, California 95076 . . . roses—old, rare and unusual, selected modern; most delightful reading. $1.

Tingle Nursery Co., Pittsville, Maryland 21850 . . . trees and shrubs, large selection, azaleas, hollies.

Marinus Vander Pol, 776 Washington Street, Fairhaven, Massachusetts 02719 . . . clematis.

Vick's Wildgardens, Box 115, Gladwyne, Pennsylvania 19035 . . . ferns and wildflowers.

Wayside Gardens, Mentor, Ohio 44060 . . . general; handsomest of catalogues; wide selection of fine varieties. Catalogue in color, $2, refundable.

White Flower Farm, Litchfield, Connecticut 06759 . . . general; excellent *Garden Book* with good cultural advice; many rarities. Catalogue in color, $2, refundable.

Gilbert H. Wild and Son, Sarcoxie, Missouri 64862 . . . perennials. 50¢.

Melvin E. Wyant, Johnny Cake Ridge, Mentor, Ohio 44060 . . . old and new roses, also Benlate. 25¢.

Index

NOTE: References to illustrations are in *italics*.